A Step Outside of Sanity

Poetic Heart

authorHOUSE®

AuthorHouse™
1663 Liberty Drive, Suite 200
Bloomington, IN 47403
www.authorhouse.com
Phone: 1-800-839-8640

© *2007 Poetic Heart. All rights reserved.*

No part of this book may be reproduced, stored in a retrieval system, or transmitted by any means without the written permission of the author.

First published by AuthorHouse 9/6/2007

ISBN: 978-1-4343-1883-1 (sc)

Library of Congress Control Number: 2007906401

Printed in the United States of America
Bloomington, Indiana

This book is printed on acid-free paper.

I dedicate this book in loving memory of the Six Piece Puzzle and my grandfather Arkady.

I want to thank all those who inspired and pushed me to write. A big thanks to Stefani, you boosted my confidence level. I want to give a special thanks to AnnMarie Papapietro a sweet and very beautiful person, I love you the warmth in the coldest times. I want to thank Lisa Gordon who made my words come out into images. A huge thank you to Cheryl and Ed Dinger two passionate roses. Thank you to my sister Irene who I love with all my heart. Thank you to a fellow artist Cynthia Nieves a supporter of my writing as I am a supporter of hers. To my family Erin, Eric, Dana, Rob, Cossie, Slad you guys are always there to make me laugh and to support me, I love you guys. To Blanca DelValle thanks for the words of wisdom, to Juan Vasquez, you inspired me, to my grandparents, concerned with love. To Jeanette "Gotchi" Accevedo I love you and thank you for the laughs, Maria Golyak, Barbara Macaluso, Cathy Latrenta, Suzanne Hroncic, and Judy Gerena thank you all for the good, to Cristain, Sharon, Vail, Steve S., Galvin, Frank, Jesse, Adam, Narendra, Pratik, Goog, Jamar, Brian D., Phil, Narali, Keri, Josh, Gabe, Svet, Casey, Michele, Jenny, and Gen, thanks for the inspirations and the good times we all had together, to the Gougliotti family, you are my family, thanks for the concern and knowledge that I have a place to go when needed. And to my Mother and Father, I wouldn't have what I have without the childhood I had.

To all those I missed, my deepest apologies,
and I will get you in the third book.

This book features two other artists,
Illustrations by Lisa Gordon
Featured poet Sadie Ryczek

Insanity comes from the heart, not the mind.

These Are The Words Of Poetic Heart

Table of Contents

Hidden Fear 1

This Is Me 2

Unconscious Night 4

Poetic Frame 5

My Muse Named Death 6

The Rallying Cry 7

The Truth Of An Artist's Stroke 9

Renewal 10

Lonely Married Man 12

Mirror Of Deception 15

Escape From Captivity 17

No Attention Paid To The Heart 20

A New Pair Of Eyes 21

The Undressed Hand 23

How Would You Feel 24

Below Her Window 25

Pebbles In Collection 26

Winter Night 28

Seventy-Five Years 29

Ghost To This World 30

Into Darkness 31

Birth And Death Of A Rose 34

Function Of A Mind 35

Floating In Nature's Arms	37
Collapsed Art	39
The Rise Of Brilliance	40
Bridge To Love	42
Night Meets Day	44
The Garden Of Winter	45
Run To The Moon	46
Portrait Of A Mind And Heart	47
Beneath Our Covers	49
Pieces Of A Puzzled Heart	52
The Beauty And Ugliness Of Life	53
A Promise On The Stars	55
Blonde Hair In Curls	56
Childhood Lost	58
Perfection	59
The Dark Lighted Path	61
Into Reflections	62
Tears In Blood	63
Two Tortured And Poetic Hearts	65
My Good Girl	67
A Sobered Story	70
Water Over Dead	74
Early Age Of War	75
Enemy Of Faith	76
Trapped In A Pocket Clock	78

After Darkness	79
The Liveethiam House	80
Hibernation Of A Mind	82
Bound To That Star	83
Street Sweeper	84
Time Lost In A Story	86
Hooded Head	87
The Shadowed Reflection	88
Love After The Grave	90
An Orphan's Tale	91
Extremity Of My Love	98
The Forbidden Leaves	99
Sisterhood	101
Rough Winds	102
An Ode Of Death	103
Snow Surrounded Cabin	105
Student In Shadow	107
Alas A Sight	109
When My Rose Was Gone	111
In Between Raindrops	112
Door	113
Flow Of Art	115
Murderous Crime	116
Wintered Lake	118
Darkened Days	120

Eyes Falling To Shadow	123
Threads	127
Battle Between Two Dragon Hearts	131
Shower Stall	133
Discussion Group	134
The Lost Legend	136
Plead	137
Letter To Heart	139
Storybook	141
Chance Meeting	143
Death Of Inspiration	149
Shadow Of A Rose	151
Little Alexes	153
Bucket Beats	156
Game In The Park	158
A Story Of Love And Hatred	159
Reading	164
Tears In Blood	166
Standing In The Rain	168
What For, I Ask	171
A Series Of Heightened Senses	173
Not My Fight	189
Library Hall	193
Stage Lighted Smile	194
A Sad Girl I Know	197

Again Silent	199
A Walk Pass Dark Doors	200
Brightest Stars	201
Read Poetry More, Never Less	202
To Silence	204
Two Way On A One Way Road	206
Gullible	207
Originality	209
The Mirror's Eyes	210
The Tall Glass	211
In The Depths Of Mid-Night	213
History	214
The Night After October 18th	215
There Was Radio	216
Hidden Wings	218
In Memory	221
Teacher	222
Test Of Talent	224
Assassination of Royalty	226
Tear Shed	228
The Roof	230
The Second's Kiss	232
Tortured Through Windows	233
The Distant Hearted	234
The Picture of Sanity and Insanity	238

Haunted Heart	239
Young Eyes	241
The Never Loving Family	243
Dead Tree, Broken Sidewalk	244
The Broken Quill	246
Framed Decisions	248
In the Shadow of the Gun	250
Out of Reach Memory	252
A Nameless Street	253
Blind Steps	254
Lured In	255
A Bright Day After a Moonless Night	256
In the Atmosphere	257
Insanity's Welcome	258
Giant And A Mouse	260
Deceptions	263
a loss of self	264
Miquela	265
nightmares	266
comfort	267
uncomfortably Numb	268
hidden treasure	269

Hidden Fear

A little boy sits at home
All alone with his purring cat,
Parents are out late again, rumbling
Flat stomach is the doormat,
Frightened little boy
Who is only seven years old,
He never gets into trouble
And does what he's told,
Parents out late partying in the love
Of the passionate night,
They leave their young son alone
In the pool of fright,
It's a fear he doesn't know how describe
Or how to explain,
It's not the darkness of the night
Followed by the thunderous rain,
His parents never take him out,
He always stays at home alone
And he's only seven years old,
He does things on his own,
Brought into a world
Not knowing he won't be cared for,
Every night he sits
Watching his parents walk, out the door,
Even though he says
He has a hidden fear
He can barely keep it in,
His so called hidden tear.

This Is Me

As I walk down the hall I get these dirty looks,
Judged like an old, dusty dirty book,
The way I dress is under attack
Oh he wants dress black,
The word wigger comes to mind,
But they wouldn't say it if they were blind,
So what if I dress thug like
I plan to move the crowd with the mike,
Said through the deeper words of my poetry
This is me,
The way that I walk
The way that I talk,
Please, read past the white cover
To find out if I'm a fighter or a lover,
These are the clothes I wear,
Don't like it, see if I care,
I like hip hop and rap
And I do think some is weak, a listener in a trap,
They rhyme about their hooked up cars
Instead of paying attention to the stars,
Say what you want, won't listen to it
Since I can walk right through it,
I can't believe this cat
Dressing like that,
He could continue with that dirty look
Looking at me, like I'm some crook
That stole, your dress style,
Check my file,
Learn to share
Stop focusing your despising stare on me,
Raised in the Bronx with hip hop,
Wake in the night from guns that pop,

Which law says which way I should dress,
Why would I want to look like a rocker's mess
Dress all preppy
Or maybe like the old school hippy,
I don't like rock n roll
For I dress my ears with soul,
It fills my heart
And no one can tare it apart,
Made out of pure steel
This is me, for real,
Watch me as I rock my head to the hip hop beat
Walking along your sight street,
Hard not to fall in love with that sound,
Put the radio down on the ground
As vibes are sent through the worldly ears,
It calms my fears
To hear the music I like
And to dress the way I like,
I don't copycat off anyone,
Don't throw it away when I'm done
For I've had this style for many years,
Now open your ears
And your mind as well
To this idea, I'm not trying to sell
Myself, don't like it, I don't really care
For this is what I wear
And this is how I walk
How I talk,
I listen to the beats of hip hop and rap,
Stand up and make it clap
Or continue with the dirty look,
Like I'm some dusty dirty book
Or a style stealing, crook?

Unconscious Night

I wake with my head throbbing
Up to my feet the strange room,
Is spinning, out of control, out of focus,
I crash back down, for I am unsure of,
Where I am, what I did, and who I did it with,
The last memory, that hasn't become a
Broken drunken, slur,
Is me, getting my last drink
Before the next moments are a blur,
Now I am in a room belonging to a stranger,
A girl that is still sleeping,
Still with her closed eyes I can not
Say that I recognize her face,
Or the strange place
That has me captive, naked,
I'm scared, my heart is pumping
Faster, to hard, what happened
When I fell unconscious to the destructive state,
Running far away from a sane state,
What did I do last night
I wish I could recall.

Poetic Frame

A poet is an artist in words
Describing the beauty of birds
In their river flowing flight,
Then there is also the ever living night
That only a true poet can put in flow,
The amounts of these poets are low,
A painter paints what he wants
As the poetic frame haunts
The mind and heart of the poet and flow of his pen,
Poetic frames were always around, even back when
Shakespeare put his words into rhyme,
Poetry's beginning time
Poetic frames were there,
As poets were in a stare
Trying to figure out how to write,
How to describe the beauty of the night
By placing it in its frame,
Look into the eyes of a poet, the flame
Going wild, but the freedom to write is not around,
To squeeze it in four lines, here that poetic sound
Living off the pen in the paper of passion,
Poets talk of their compassion
To have sixteen lines in a flow,
No rhyme, but the story will flow,
No syllable pattern, but their is a flow,
Deep expression and it has a flow,
Describing the sunset in a certain flow,
Doesn't fit in the frame, but it has a flow
That's the poet's artistic mind
That was able to unwind.

My Muse Named Death

What is it about death
That puts my writing into effect,
The feeling of loosing someone,
Can't write a word without death,
Funny to say death, is my inspiration
My muse is named death,
When someone looses their breath
When their eyes grow cold
My best work comes out,
The grim reaper attacks in the shadows
Words start to flow,
The pen stays motionless
But as soon as a life is taken
The paper fills up with my passion,
Words I never knew
I had lingering around in my head,
My inspiration to write
My need to get the pen flowing
But this time without my muse death,
Unfortunately death, gets these ideas going,
Open eyes, a cold run,
No one has died
No one has cried,
The obituaries are dry from death
And everyone continues to blink,
My paper is empty of words,
My muse can not be found in the low shadows,
When a body is cold
My words will then, start to flow
And until then, enjoy the life you have.

The Rallying Cry

Put a stop to this
No one lives a life in mythical bliss,
You can hear it in the rallying cry
That no one likes to say goodbye,
A rally against death,
A rally to save that innocent breath,
Crowd of people giving their support
Standing in the cold outside an unfair court,
Wondering what's the ruling against the innocent man,
Guilty, rest of his life in a tight can
With a murderer that wants to rape him,
Uh oh, lights growing dim,
The next rally is this
Happiness is in a miss,
Tried to get it into their life
Overwhelmed by strife,
Disillusions of a fair rule,
But the reality is the world, is cruel
And nothing can stop it, he'll die
Still ears hear the rallying cry,
The world is unjust
And smiles are a must,
We rally for those who believe
Not for those who pack up and leave,
Behind their falsehood
Of what could
Be, a fair place,
No one judged from the cover of their face,
But sadly, nothing has changed
Nothing rearranged
So here comes the rallying cry,
And I wonder why

That poor man should walk in restraints
For all know he caused no one pain,
To death of a nice guy
Oh you'll hear our rallying cry
To set him free
From your cruel and unjust world, he'll flee
Into the wide open arms of a better life,
Without that planted knife,
Now here is this situation I went through
For believe it true,
Me, a white kid
And my friend, a black kid,
We were just walking down the street
With new sneakers on our feet,
A cop comes up to us
As we were about to get on the bus,
Asked, no, told my friend to step to the side,
We missed our ride
Just because he looked "suspicious", like he might have stole,
I stood waited by the bus pole,
I couldn't take it, I started the rallying cry
For the unjust act to die,
My rally attracted so many more,
Walked out their door
To join in on letting the young kid free
And now I again, I attract with a rally.

The Truth Of An Artist's Stroke

On the floor at the end of a long hall
Lies a covered painting,
Painted by a brilliant artist
Who is now gone from this world,
Many think that painting, sits incomplete,
But only one knows the truth
Behind its covers
The truth behind his stroke,
It is the truth of the artist's stoke,
Who decides what the artist wants
What he wants us to think
Us to feel
When we see his painting,
No instructions are ever left,
No words describing what the artist painted,
They stayed with in his heart when he died
Sharring it with no one,
His final painting is kept at the end of a long hall
Where all his paintings are kept,
A collection of his work
An event to uncover,
A shock given to the world
When shown the artist's stroke,
A single stroke
Many think it brilliant work.

Renewal

A couple married for almost thirty years
And they hardly shed any tears,
Their love is dry,
For all are asking why,
It's the day they celebrate when they wed,
Thirty years since their vows were said
And their love is not the same anymore,
Divided by a stiff locked door,
Their love has dried,
Only said on a untouched cup
That he once gave to her,
But now that day is a constant blur
And all that she gets is a cold touch,
She misses that blurred day so much
That she falls asleep to dream it,
Their love candle is no longer lit
No longer can it be seen
For now grows space in-between,
She comes home that day
With something new to say,
The house is empty of light
For it can be mistaken for night,
She opens the front door
And finds rose petals spread on the floor,
She stands there with a confused look,
At the end of the path lies a book
In it contained a poem he wrote,
Written in a rhyme note
And it was addressed to his love of thirty years,
Their song, the key, heard by her ears,
She follows the sound downstairs
And finally love flares

Ignited by a strong source,
Their love has no planed course,
Since their love was dried
Many thought it just died,
But it's him for her and her for him,
Their love has and never will fall dim.

Lonely Married Man

To be lonely is to be by yourself,
A book resting on a dusty shelf,
See I know this married man
Who lives the best way he can,
Still he feels lonely
Reaching out saying hold me
To his wife, two kids, and cat,
His life is flat
Never going above zero,
He wants to be a hero
In the eyes of his kids and wife
But they hardly acknowledge his life,
He feels lonely with all these people around him
As he stands in a light that is going dim,
He looks to the right
And sees a loving family, a lonely sight
Since he has that without love
In the everyday life, excuse me, shove
That was his friend
And now he feels worse, an end
To the loneliness he feels, look to the left,
The night in theft,
Does he realize
How to be a hero in their eyes,
Loneliness will end
And not to be lost to his friend
Who just runs by
Goodbye,
His wife walks in to the bedroom, no hi
Goodbye,
His kids walk through ignoring a cry
Goodbye,

To finally go above zero
All he wants it be loved, considered a hero
By the people he cares for,
He turned the lights off, closed the door
And it is a beautiful sight from above
For he left, his wife and kids lost, in the absence of his love.

Mirror Of Deception

When you look into a mirror, what do you see,
When I look, I think if it is truly
Me,
Or what I want it to be,
Or is it what you perceive
Truth, your eyes can't receive
The mirror loves to deceive,
To tease the eyes of a fool,
The mirror lives during four years of high school,
It shows two people as friends
The truth is what the mirror hunts, to bend,
They stay close till school ends
For they go their separate ways, living their life,
Reaching for the back stabbing knife
A mirrored blade of deception,
All seek acception
Into the popular world, a reflection,
The popular world diminishes after those years
Never showing true tears
Hiding everyone's true fears,
The mirror shattered before graduation day
Me and my so called friend, went our separate ways,
So I stand there thinking I know, supposedly knew
What was true
So who are you
Standing in front of the mirror of deception
Can I make that connection
Between me, and who stands, in the reflection,
As it shines onto the web
With the spider dangling down at the ebb
Looking at who truly stands there,
The ones who might care

Are the friends who stick around
The ones that paid attention, to the crying sound
For the pieces of the mirror lie on the ground,
Life is easier to live
Advice is easier to give
When truth is seen by my eyes,
No more lies
Deception finally dies.

Escape From Captivity

There is a life on the other side of these bars,
Through the spaces I can see the stars,
Born in captivity, I have no choice
For I have no voice
To demand to be free,
Instead I sit under a plastic tree,
People come to stare,
Cross these bars no one will dare
For on the other side people live
Advice to help, they itch to give,
The excitement of their life
Survival from strife
And the freedom to fall in love,
Fear of a turn away shove,
There is good and bad
Happy and the sad,
What crime did I commit to deserve this,
This is hell, not bliss,
Unhappy in here
For can't you see my tear,
I want to run
Is captivity done,
Escape from their hold,
I want to feel the cold
I want to feel the warmth of another,
But why bother,
They'll never let me go
Never will I see the river flow,
Also, I won't feel hurt
And be treated like I was lower than dirt,
Never experience heart ache,
A dive into love, never will I take,

Never will I be able to do such a thing,
I hear the alarm ring
Out in the wild, I'm free
Gone from captivity,
Its all just a dream
Wake up from a baby's scream,
They'll never let me go on my own,
For I have grown
Sitting behind these bars
Never on the other side of the stars,
My eyes see routine every day of the year,
I sit there and strike fear
Into the eyes of a crying baby
People saying I'm lazy,
Oh yea right, let me run around the can,
Only way I feel winter is by a fan
Blowing on high,
My roar is my cry
To be set loose,
Can't tie a rope into a noose,
I want to run
To feel the heat of the summer's sun,
All I feel is the UV light
Inside during the winter night,
Can you hear my cry to be free
To escape from captivity,
Let me go on my own,
Hear my lonely tone,
My roar does not strike fear, it feels fear,
For I feel like a defenseless dear,
Everyone on the outside has it good
Living fancy, or in the hood,
They get to live
Love they can give

To someone of undeniable beauty
While I'm stuck in captivity,
For this day and the next,
Here is my text.

No Attention Paid To The Heart

People say follow your heart,
Even if it is torn apart
Would it still be the same, pain
All caught in the throat of the drain,
Would ears be open
Ready to listen to something broken
Not once, twice, but six times,
Can you hear the broken chimes
Wondering truth of her excuse,
Her heart never in use
For her touch was cold,
Love's call put on hold,
I rather listen to my mind
For my heart is blind,
Why listen to a feeble muscle
Lacking strength to hustle,
Why listen to feeling, when there is no reason,
I hate love's season
Couples kissing in the park
Until fall brings the dark,
Can a heart mend completely leaving no pain,
Happiness is measured in a grain,
A busted bubble
Is a heart of this body, it stands double,
One side stays true to itself
Even if it's a book on a dusty shelf,
The other side holds my pain
And tears,
It conquers my fears,
Sometime you have to listen to the heart,
Even if, it is torn apart.

A New Pair Of Eyes

My eyes use to see the world, in a different way,
I use to act so different
For I stepped to the hardcore beat,
I was able to stand up and curse
Strait into the eyes of this world
Asking why life is so distraught, and chaotic,
Why is this world blind
To those lower than the high,
Then came a pair of new eyes
That changed me,
The way I see things
The way I see the world,
Rainy days, meant to keep me out of trouble
Still living, close to the bursting bubble,
Alive I stand, to see her have a life,
For my love goes to her
All of it,
One love to my baby girl
For my eyes will never be the same.

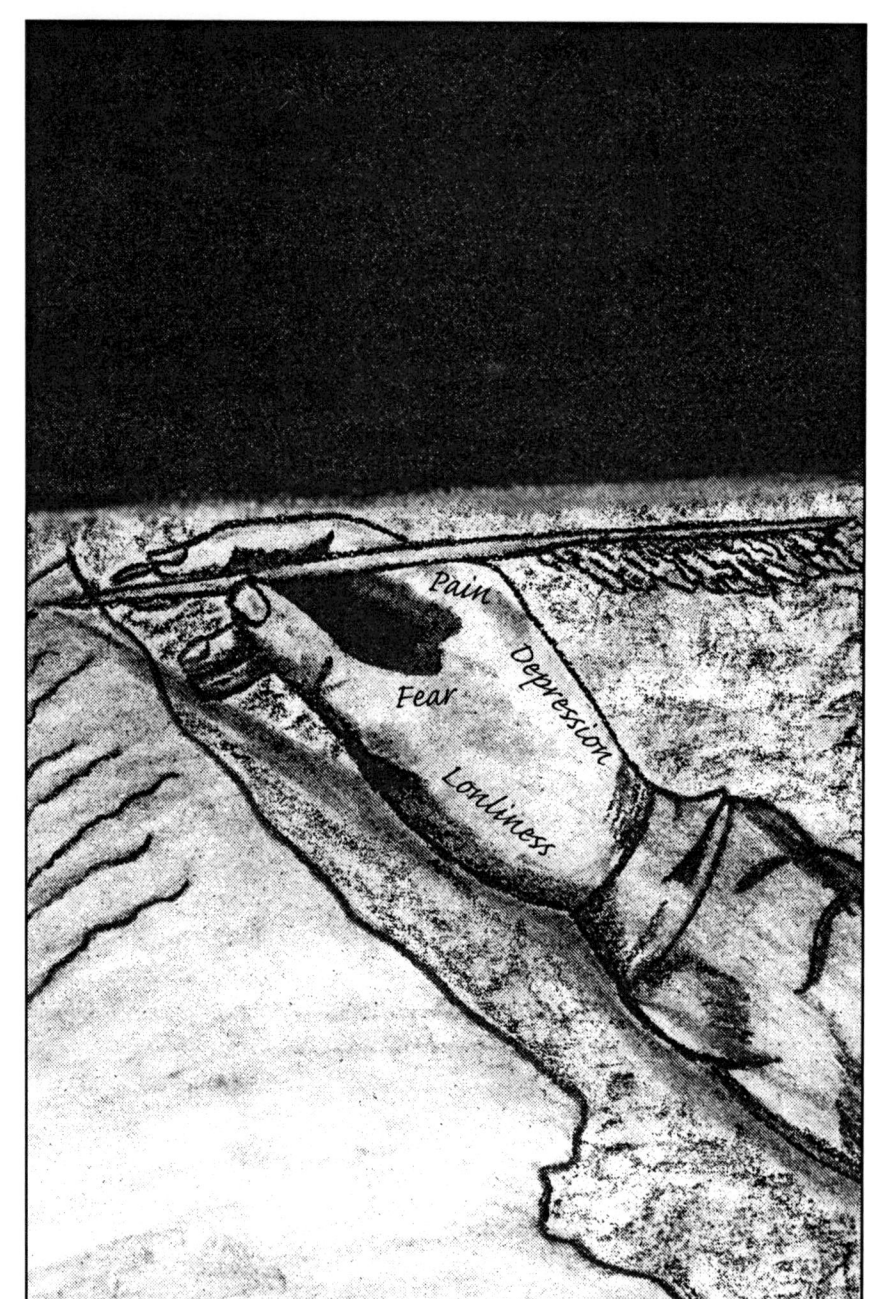

The Undressed Hand

My feelings expressed, not through the mouth
But through the written word,
I can only open up with a pen
For my vocal words won't make sense,
My hand, can tell the past
As well as speak my voice,
Putting words on paper
Is not that easy
Expression of how I feel,
My heart and mind collaborate
While my hand puts the finishing touch,
Can't use my voice to tell a girl hello
For it is my hand that describes the poetic flow,
I am like this since birth
For now I use my hand to express this Earth,
But read deeper, into my words
And you will see
My hand is all that I have
To speak my mind,
And to speak my vocal heart.

How Would You Feel

Broken Promises, uttered through a broken voice,
Two reserved seats stay empty,
Words of discouragement
For why encourage me to do something I love,
Put me down to the ground,
The whip of a belt
But if you can imagine, worse pain is felt
For how would you feel
If the two people that brought you in
Don't care to be there,
Not even to stand up, and cheer,
Never think to say
How proud they are of me,
Instead, they feel cheated
Out of a better son,
Never did I drink, smoke, and kill
But still
I'm a bad son,
I try my best
They want me to be above the best,
Strait A's,
It's just not me,
How would you feel
If words of anger, are thrown at you
Never told of a dying love,
Until it was too late,
How would you feel.

Below Her Window

Below her window grows
A beautiful rose,
Only there during the late night,
During the day, it's not in sight,
It comes out to catch her eye
For it will always grow, never will it die,
Another night, there's the rose
No matter how strong the wind blows,
How cold the nights get
The rose will not leave, it is set
Until she picks it,
The rose will sit
Growing with every passing night,
Only to be in her sight.

Pebbles In Collection

Memories can be reminded in the smallest
Of things,
A pebble found right after a first kiss
Or a hurtful expression of feeling,
My mind slips deeper, loosing sight
Of those certain memories
That I would like to remember,
A bag I hold close to me filled
With a collection of little pebbles,
I don't want to forget people and the times
We all had together, their laughs
Their next word, my love,
She caught the attention of my eyes
And we talked for hours, laughing
And just having a good time,
I have that pebble in my collection,
A kiss between me and my first love
And I lost her, both pebbles in my collection,
This is all that I have of my life,
Certain things I can't, will never recall
For my memory is being eaten alive,
I take a pebble, rub it and I feel
And live the memory in dream,
I lost all the people that I care,
For, I out lived them all
And to see them again, before my death,
I reach in to my bag, in dream
I see, the one that makes me feel
The one that makes me smile
The one that can make me freeze
Forget my name, age, and who I am,
Another pebble please

For I want to see my son, daughter, daughter,
Oh, and my other two sons,
Let me see, let me hear them
In my dreams when I close my eyes
With my magical pebble in hand
That brings me back to that moment
That I picked up, that memory pebble,
Kept alive, in the bag that gives it air
Gives it the magic from the moon,
The moment will be kept in the eye of the pebble
Thunder, in the eye, never loosing the night
Never loosing the strike of the moment,
Hours of recording time,
I reach into the ocean, pull out the pebble,
The ocean is deepened
By the hurt I felt,
The ocean is the life of me,
But I feel lost in it, without my collection
Of every single of my hundreds of pebbles.

Winter Night

Stretch my hands, to the winter sky
Feeling free in the winter night, no lie,
Leave all my troubles behind
For its gone, from my mind
In the open air
Without a single care,
Floating up to the winter star,
Is really not that far
For it might look like, too much
But, the winter night holds, and gives the touch
To put you in sleep,
And fall in deep
Of the winter night, winter night take my life
And give me one, in that starry sky, with no strife,
Ready, for the darkness of the night,
I'm walking toward, that winter light.

Seventy-Five Years
To my Grandmother and Great Uncle

Let me tell you a story
For believe it true,
Seventy five years ago, two people were born
In a world that was about to be torn,
A world was at war
As two hearts stand in the shadows of a door,
Our relatives and friends, watch war break
For they feel heart ache,
Seeing tears, on young faces,
Them showing fear on their faces
Looking out into a world of tears
A world of fears,
They flee under the moon's bright glow
To escape in the night's shadow,
A grandmother, mother, wife, and sister shows tears,
A grandfather, father, husband, and brother shows tears,
Still they bravely run to safety,
Safe they shall be
The survivors of strife,
We celebrate their continuing life
As we toast to their seventy fifth year,
We celebrate their laughter, not tear,
A story of my grandmother and great uncle's escape way,
We're here to celebrate their birthday
To show our continuing love toward them
This is to the surviving hearts of war,
Surviving hearts of life.

Ghost To This World

My footsteps can not be heard
Nor can they be seen,
I don't exist to the eyes of the world
But I do walk past them,
I am a ghost to this world
Yet the world, is not a ghost to me
For I see the wrongs of the world,
Don't bother to correct, for my actions are translucent,
My lucid word, gone from all ears,
How can a man who wasn't there
Break someone's heart
And force tears from their eyes,
To force cries
How can I express my love to her
If my words are mute,
How can a man who wasn't there
Tell her, she is all I need,
I bleed in love, for her
But it doesn't matter,
For no one knows, that I walk these streets,
I sit alone in a crowd of empty seats,
I know how it was to be heard
How it felt to be seen
And talked to,
I am in the dark endless night
Even in the brightest light
I am in the only shadow,
If I don't exist, why am I still here
Living my greatest fear,
Whatever I do
However loud I shout,
I walk about
A ghost, to this world.

Into Darkness

Just the beginning of this war,
Innocence is spread all over the battlefield floor,
Darkness, is in the color of red
In the road of the dead,
A name given from the sight,
An endless night
Where bodies fill the street,
Boulders of concrete
Hold up some of the lifeless innocent,
Yea, to a better place they were sent
But they didn't deserve to die,
On this cold dark floor, they lie
Pieces of buildings hold their blood
Rolling into the street in a flood,
Step into the darkness of this place,
See frozen fear on innocent's face
Nowhere safe from the bullet, into death
That holds your breath,
Step after step, going deeper in,
Where are the bodies filled with sin,
Why are they not lying in everlasting darkness,
Innocence fight, for they are told to,
Darkness is what they fall to,
Attacked from every side
And another innocent died
For the pointless cause of this war,
Shut that open door
Safety is no longer seen,
Shocked, frozen, execution of a teen,
Close range shot to the head
Darkness splattered in the color, red,
When do we see the end,

They force innocence, to make their knees bend,
Onto the blood covered floor
With one shot, they are out of the war,
Step into darkness, and see
Everyone running for safety
In the chapel, it's not a vacant dome,
Explosion through a child's bedroom, no one's home,
Crowded streets of lifeless bodies and ruble,
A bullet burst the protective bubble,
At the end of the long path of red
Lies a little boy, dead,
Step further into darkness and see
The little boy is me.

Birth And Death Of A Rose

Birth is given tonight,
Life is brought into sight
This is the birth of a rose,
With eyes open in a pose,
To stay open, to the pain,
Tears coming down like rain
Also open to the smiles of life,
Trying not to pay attention to strife
All those around only feel its lonely touch,
For it is felt too much,
Not knowing when to look,
Truth can come out of a book
That one rose will focus our eyes
Not on the depressing sounds and sights of cries,
But on the smiles, of a face,
That face is in the rose's birth place
Where the happiness of the sun
And the tears of the dark sky, have a son,
A rose that is born to light
But never to forget the night,
For we need both to survive
And to feel alive
In our hearts, minds, and souls,
To mend our hearts full of holes
We give birth to a life,
And wait for the death, of strife.

Function Of A Mind

How does a mind bring so much to life
Giving images seen, in his head,
Or words thought
Of and brought
To the living paper,
Using our eyes to read what they said
That life without tears
Is no life at all,
To experience life
We must experience pain,
Walk down a dim hall
Vibrant colors of a painter's stroke,
Seeing the world through their eyes
Bringing it onto canvas,
We see their world of smiles and cries,
A writer explains his world
Through symbols, tricks of the written word,
And vibrant expression,
We see their world
We see what they heard,
The way the mind gives light
To the darkest corner of a shadow,
Through the fog of darkness
Comes the brightest glow,
What gives a mind inspiration to write a sunset
Or even pain the night blue,
It is the pain of life
The torture of a heart,
Is to make it true,
To experience happiness, experience pain,
The mind can not be fit
To bring his world into focus,

Into the reality of the paint,
To bring their world, into light
Into the reality of word, it's faint,
No pain to feel
No truths to see, hear, or read,
A needed element in the mind
Is the tortured seed,
The mind puts reality in front of you,
Open your eyes, to find the world,
It might be hard,
But find truth in word
Through the function of your mind
Through the written word,
The painted sight,
Or the sung love.

Floating In Nature's Arms

Down come tears of the sky,
Soaking a world that has run dry,
Refreshing, the eyes of, the young
A tree, has been hung,
Innocent or not
It was caught in its still spot,
Floating, in the arms of nature, is death,
Reviving it giving it new breath
To see, and to hear life of new,
Here is a life so true,
Tears of the sky so cold, it is frozen coming down
Hitting the heart of this little town,
Wondering when, it will finally end,
The touch of a friend,
Snowflakes float down to the ground,
Making not even the slightest sound,
A silent kill
The world sits still,
Tears of the sky fall
Refreshing the eyes of all,
Hearts do mend to this,
It is nature in bliss
To where new petals wake,
A chance at love shall take
Happiness of the sun, floats in nature's arm
Protecting it from harm,
Smiles are seen all around
Listen to that laughing sound,
Can this actually, be true,
That the world is gone from blue,
No, it's around
Just sleeping, under the laughing sound,

Waiting for a chance, to teach,
Another heart to breach,
Life's lesson spoken through rain,
Season's of floating pain,
Can you describe, what you learn
Before you rest in a coffin, or an urn,
Speechless, every time,
Lips sealed from a bitter lime,
No need, to pay attention, for it'll be caught,
No need to find you, it won't sought
You out, for you'll come to nature's arms,
Don't run, just hear the jingle of the floating charms,
It's not your place to say
For life's lesson is on its way.

Collapsed Art

A masterpiece, hangs on a wall
Showing, complexities of life, to any eyes
That can bare,
To just stand, and stare
Deep into the eyes of red,
A masterpiece within another
Showing reality's true color,
No one can pass it, without a look,
Colors of how the world was shook
By the controversial, reality,
That the artist had expressed,
A crowd appears
Protesting, that the beauty should not disappear,
Only to forever be on display,
How can it be
That is not, what I see,
My eyes find, the reality of the picture,
In a rough texture
The masterpiece within,
Is in a destructed color,
No more expression
No more passion,
Where has the beauty disappeared to,
No more red, no more blue,
It happens to be
That darkness, comes over beauty.

The Rise Of Brilliance

Once in every million, true brilliance can rise
To bring, understanding to all confused eyes,
If you're lucky, two shall appear
To tragically disappear,
Many will disagree with billions,
Even if they march against the wise in millions,
They can take away those words, in an instant,
Be carried off somewhere, distant,
Never again will you hear, the words from his mind,
That brings images of beauty, to the blind,
Take a look, up at the sky
That is expressive to me, you know why
There are true believers
And the hardcore disbelievers,
The hard headed deceivers
And light hearted receivers
Of the true brilliance of life,
Knowing your need, of strife,
To learn that life, is trial and error
To smile all the time, never
Do we feel misery and pain,
For we smile when we see, the falling rain,
Brilliance knows, that it's apart of life,
You and me, are not in fault,
Life is pain, happiness assault,
Rev. Martin Luther King Jr. knew that,
I read his passionate words under a dusty mat,
The rise of brilliance and the fall,
Something I would love to stall,
And for every decision we make
To teach us life in smile, and pain,
For you can still smile in the rain,

Keep eyes open to the sky
Never asking why,
For you did not pay attention to your misery,
From it you'll learn, trust me,
Brilliance can come at any time
For it be in rhyme
Or strait forward, no disguise,
Just open your closed, eyes.

Bridge To Love

I walk from one side to another,
Step after step, getting closer
To a heart, I don't know
Over the river's flow,
Where pain of a broken heart, reaches out,
For it shouts,
Give yourself into her smile,
She is not like the other
Who used a heart, to tare it apart,
Left nothing but a hole,
Blowing winds from a storm
It can't hold me back,
For I keep taking step after step,
Getting closer
No cracks or shaken steel,
On this bridge, to the other side,
The storm has died,
It's easier to take that step,
Easier to give in,
Not being afraid, of hurt,
For fear lies twenty feet, under the dirt
And the river's flow,
I let go.

Night Meets Day

The rays of a new day meet, with a pair
Of haunted panes,
In the elegance of a cool night breeze,
Sits a shivering soul
That can't bear, the dark nights.

Stains on the black carpet, coming from
An open slit, done in a single moment
When sunset, convened with moonrise
And there stood the balance,
There was simplicity in chaos,
For when the cruelty of day
And fear of night, came together
There rose peace from the graveyard,
A moment, in the midst of waste,
The best view is on top, of the laughing face
Stoned, kept laughing at the seconds passing,
But smiling, when night meets day,
There sits the shivering soul, frozen
In the anticipation of that flash,
Hand held firmly against his wrist,
Hoping for some ease.

The Garden Of Winter

The cold pale sun
Sits in the arms of the bitter sky,
While the rose misses the warmth,
Another flower grows from the cold
Feeding off the darkness of the winter sky,
It lives while others die,
This flower grins at death
Not afraid to take a final breath,
Saying that there is nothing left,
The garden of winter, is a darkened step,
A path of fallen leaves
Leads, up to this flower,
Where it sits on a throne,
Bring upon this world
The bitter touch of a hand,
Sticking seeds under the snowy white sand,
A garden filled with these flowers
Where the cold touch of winter
Is far from this garden,
A flower that takes the life, of others,
But the heat, of the burning sun,
Can tear off its petals
For when, light out
It sits in the darkness,
Of its own company,
The flower of the undead,
Sits inside the blood of darkness,
For winter brings a dim sun,
Protecting the light are eyes
That sits, in the head of the flower.

Run To The Moon
Inspired by Jeanette "Gotchi" Accevedo

Escape from this life
Just to run away
And never turn back,
Run, towards the moon
And have my back, turned on the sun,
I want to run
Away, from guns that kill
Away, from a life that is frozen, still
Held back, by overprotective hands
That are not, that protective
Since I am being held back
From experiences,
Back from pieces of a broken heart
Something that can make me stronger
Still I live, this life
With my heart in pieces,
I escaped for a while
To try on a smile,
I escaped into love, on the first try
That's why, I see the moon cry,
Why those hands try to protect me,
Till the end, the day I die,
But I want to escape
Once again, into love
Where I can be happy,
Or at least, content in the living,
But the only way I can do this,
Is if I run, towards the moon
And have my back, turned at the sun,
I need to escape into love.

Portrait Of A Mind And Heart

Close your eyes, and picture,
Picture an apartment building, in the color gray,
Twenty five stories high, tall, standing,
Sitting on a sidewalk in Manhattan,
Halls, are painted gray
And freshly installed, gray carpeting,
At the end, of the hall is 25D,
Enter through the door,
Look down, body lies on the floor,
Still breathing, but cold,
He lies there still
On his gray, ruined, rug,
Thinking about what happened,
His mind clashed, with his heart
Here, is a man that never felt
The warmth of a woman's touch
Or the warmth of her smile,
His mind, did all of that for him
Making up stories, in his head,
Giving him a false pretence
In his mind, he is happy
But in his heart,
Despair and a dim light
Hangs over it,
One day he finds someone
That likes him, and he likes her,
What's the problem, well
The mind is not happy,
One can't be happy, without the other
For the mind is not making any stories,
No more false pretences,
The mind sit gloaming

While the heart is glowing,
An evil grin, is on his mind,
For a story is made up
Of, there are better out there,
The heart weighs heavy
Scared, falling tears
Falling into fears
Of a possible broken muscle,
The heart begged him not to listen
For life is too good
To happy is he now, without a mirage,
Now that she has come in,
No attention was paid to the heart
As the body lies cold,
Picture a mind at ease, and whole,
Then paint another picture
In your own heart,
Of another heart
In pain, and in shattered pieces,
Go back to the apartment,
His heart lies
In that bottle,
Pick him up, and let him
Drink his heart back in.

Beneath Our Covers

Madness
Mayhem,
People screaming
People yelling,
Hearts are breaking,
Bodies still aching,
Nine to five
With a few hours of OT,
Stressful steps
And quick decisions,
Heads pounding, from the busy streets,
Tick tock, tick tock,
Millions of people on one city block
Moving in opposite directions
Step after step,
Word after word
Too many sounds, are heard,
The day is over
The clock has gone around,
Fewer feet on the ground,
Teeth are brushed
Alarms are set
Towels are wet,
All are under their covers,
All are calm beneath,
All are at ease,
Just because their covered,
They are in their beds
Under their covers,
Eyes are closed to the world,
Hearts are under their covers,
Worry no more

As problems lie dead on the floor,
Covered by material,
That we see as
Our protection
That takes away our fear,
Our headaches,
Our worries, of this world,
That we can't let go
In dream, blocked river flow,
In our dreams, the impossible
Is always possible,
For all are asleep,
Beneath their covers.

Pieces Of A Puzzled Heart

Emotions running wild,
Pieces of a heart piled
Up to the highest star,
Thousands of pieces of a jigsaw scar,
Who to turn to, where to dream,
Pain is the river's fast stream,
Each piece of that heart
Holds a puzzled emotion, every part,
Every single speck of that heart's vein,
Piece by piece, this heart starts to form,
Coming together as of it was, a raging storm,
Feeling fear and sadness, all at the same time,
Tears fighting, through the grime,
At the sight of mixed emotions,
Felt deep, within the oceans,
Of many puzzled hearts,
Trying to find, their pieces, their parts.

The Beauty And Ugliness Of Life

The beauty of the midnight sky
And the ugliness, of a murdered ten year old boy,
Both can happen, within the same crack of time,
Within one drop of a dime
Both can also be seen by, covered eyes,
Just now, being brought out from lies,
A ten year old boy, dies,
Stars imbedded, in the midnight sky
Giving a glow, to the midnight fly,
Ugliness can not be something, you can run away from,
Every street, homeless crawl for a crumb,
Every crumb sleeps on the street,
All hearts feel some sort of pain,
Blind see the coldness, of the streets, with a cane,
Ugliness all around,
From skyscrapers to the underground,
Knives enter, innocent bodies and hearts,
Hands tearing them apart
As tears fall from a single mother,
Been with one man, and no other,
In a world that is so mean
Ugliness can be seen,
But once in a while, stars are in sight
In a star filled midnight,
Pass the moon, are the rolling clouds of gray
That strikes romance, in the month of May,
Shut your eyes, and dream,
Ignore that shout, ignore that scream,
Fluttering eyes, picture the beauty of life,
Not dreaming, of the stress, of strife,
But of snowfall, covering the ugly street,
Melting cold acts from the summer heat,

Behind the shadow
Is beauties glow,
The smiles and pain
The sunshine and rain,
Ugliness of this life
Is pain and strife,
Beauty is that star
Seen from a far,
The touch of love
With no turn away shove,
Mystics in the waterfall mist
Beauty in a million page list,
Ugliness is behind the shadow
As beauty is in the river's flow,
An invitation to her heart,
Beauty is in the middle and start
For there is no room, for ugliness.

A Promise On The Stars

The sun closes its eyes,
As the moon opens its,
A bright glow
In the middle of night's window,
A heart tells another
That he loves no other,
He promises, on the stars,
The ones near and far
Left and right,
North and south
And on a clear night
Or on a night, where clouds overrule,
On the tiny ones
And on that big one,
That he loves her
The reflection of the midnight sky
In her left, and right eye,
Those stars are hers,
The ones she sees
And the ones she can't,
He loves her and no other heart,
He promises, on the stars.

Blonde Hair In Curls

A father and his little princess,
She takes away his stress
With every smile,
He would go that extra mile
For his little girl
Blonde hair in curls,
She is at the age of thirteen,
Eyes so green,
She is daddy's little girl
Still has, her blonde hair in curls,
He takes her on a fair ride
On the boat's right side,
Away from the crowd
There comes, the covering gray cloud,
Not his dream to have a girl
With blonde hair in curls,
She tales away his stress, in more than one way,
A smile, and a friendly shake, you can say.
Mother doesn't know a thing
As he gives her presents, like a sparkling ring
And a beautiful new dress,
For his darling, little princess,
Years have pass
Distorted memory through the drinking glass,
Words of shock, hit the grown up princess,
Feelings she tried to suppress
But from the death of her darling father,
And the jealous feel, of a battered mother,
For her daughter, only felt his touch,
She didn't care for her, well being and such,
It was the attention and love
She received from the one, up above,

Princess's blonde hair, now black,
Her mind under too much attack,
By the past
Of her father, that did not last,
In his eight by four cage,
He has folded his own page.

Childhood Lost

A heart that grew up too fast,
Childhood was of the far off past,
Mature heart at the age of ten,
The death of two men
Eyes focus in on a world of sin,
Death comes into sight, of his eyes,
His childhood dies
Growing up in a neighborhood of crime,
Where church bells fear to chime,
A ten year old heart
Sees two men's deathly depart,
Right there, in front of him
He sees, death's smile so grim,
No more childhood at play,
An endless summer day
For his heart now has a different beat,
One not made of concrete
For it changed, at the sight of death,
Two men's final breath,
Lost childhood at the darkened death sight
In the darkness of the night,
In the deepest darkest shadow
Beyond the reach, of the moon's glow,
A ten year old, heart lost its innocent, young,
Childhood let out to dry, it was hung.

Perfection

World is not perfect
World is not this,
Now we don't live in a world of bliss
Where things just get handed to you,
Shocked, surprised
That you might have to work
For what you want,
Yea well, get used to it
Because without some hustle
You won't get to where you want,
Give me a break with that game show
For you won't get the respect
But you might get the deal,
Fifteen minutes of fame
It's just a game
That they play with you,
You're going to be the biggest,
Stop, please let me do it on my own,
For now that is just the hype,
Grow with the years
To learn
And earn
The respect of those
Who worked to get
Where they are,
Go from show to show
Trying to make it big,
Send in your mix tape,
Manuscript,
Demo,
Sample, whatever you want,
Just know that without some hustle,

Nothing is going to happen,
So pickup your head and
Look down the road
And walk it,
No shortcut for they lead
To termination of the mind and heart,
Step one and two
Did that flower naturally grow
And was there some flick
Of the magic trick,
Perfection doesn't live in this place,
You'll experience set backs
And pushes, shoves,
Leave, don't give up,
In dreams, what would happen,
Push back,
Lean forward,
Stop the closing door,
Sing,
Write,
Paint,
Rap,
Dance,
Do it, do it now,
Don't let up
Don't sit down
Just because the world
Is not perfection,
The world is not this,
We have to fight for bliss.

The Dark Lighted Path

How can it be
That deep down inside of me,
I feel the pain of another
Not my blood relative, not my brother,
I stand looking down
Pain echoing off the walls of this town,
Blood vessels run around,
The heart plays that musical sound,
And there I am standing over him,
Life light going dim,
Gun barrel smoking up, into the night air,
Into his closed eyes, I couldn't help but stare,
Ever since I was ten
I've been in the shadow, of criminal men,
Walking down the dark lighted path,
Many innocent people felt my dark wrath,
Killed my first at the early age,
Loyal friends kept, me out of a cage
That could have helped, my life,
Which wouldn't have ended with a knife,
My path could have been bright
Instead, I stayed within the night
Fighting off the moon's glow,
Can't see it through the window
My one good friend,
Showed me my path's end,
A close to this life's letter,
Without me, it's better.

Into Reflections

He sees his reflection in her eyes
A watering, vision in cries,
Next to her, his heart lies,
He starts to tell her
Everything is in blur,
For only she is in sight,
Only she, has him during day and night.

She looks at him
As the room's light grows dim,
As the night's clouds are trim,
She holds him ever so tight,
Knowing, that he means his words,
The light is dark,
And silence, is unheard of
As she promises the same,
Looking into his eyes,
A reflection of her tears in his.

Tears In Blood

The sound of a slamming door
Echoes through out the buildings hallways,
Over and over again,
Moonlight shines in through the window
Onto a bath of tears,
Slowly soaking into the bed
Straining strait through the protective sheets,
Tears drop to a snowfall's style,
Feather like, but stained red,
Speculation of what occurred
Varied in words,
Whether it was under the spell of the moon
Or in the fiery passion of the sun,
The bath of tears lingered round
Never completely soaking dry into the bed,
The one body was stained with agonizing pain
For tears poured out like a river drain,
But still they're stained in red,
Tears come seeping out of the eye
That leads to a heart
And that goes back up to the mind,
What is there, hidden in dormant
Until the clap of thunder
And it's awake,
What is it when someone has no more tears,
Does it mean no fears,
Absolutely no worries,
A heart stays empty of snow flurries,
Or have they all been drained out,
All that is left is the current
Of the body's river,
Pumping throughout the eyes,

Heart and its mind,
All that is left is blood,
Killing the body of love
Loosing its blood because of the lack of tears,
Killing that body of admiration
Slowly or in a quick pace
Do those blood tears
Pour out onto the bed,
The eyes still has tears to shed,
But cries out tears in blood instead
Staining her comfort,
Whether under the spell of the moon
Or in the fiery passion of the sun
Those tears stain, soak, they stay.

Two Tortured And Poetic Hearts

Two heats lay in bed,
One heart's eyes, grows with water
Streaming down
Ending, on the left side of her frown,
Right there he promises, not to leave
To stay with her,
Time doesn't matter
For the whole world could shatter,
He would still smile
As long as she is there,
She could, make him feel that way,
Where she, is all he sees,
No reason remains,
No reason alive, for him to leave
He wants to be with her,
A never ending romance
For two tortured and poetic hearts.

My Good Girl

Two little girls in their bunk beds
In their room
In their house
In a world,
One is five,
The other is eight,
One sleeps
Dreams of candy
And, endless laughing,
The other sits up
Tears bucketing down, from the top bunk,
Holding her doll
Petting its head,
Repeating good girl, good girl, good girl, my good girl,
I feel her tears,
Raindrops, from gray eyes,
For whatever reason
She sheds her cries
Onto my, humanlike hair,
Silence echoes through
For just, her tears break through,
And her shrivel little voice
Saying, good girl, good girl, good girl, my good girl,
She laid me on the bed
Beside her,
From here, I can describe her,
A river running down her face,
Red spots all around
As she tries to wipe away,
Her tears of sadness,
She gets under the covers
And holds me tight,
Still eyes open

Letting tears run
Up from her heart
Soaking red spots, that sizzle,
And she keeps saying, good girl, good girl, good girl, my good girl,
She came home,
Ran up the stairs
Having some sort
Of great news,
Entered her room,
Picked me up
Said, "hey good girl
Guess what?"
I stayed quiet,
You know, since my lips are shut
Made out of wax,
I'm a doll,
I can't talk,
She continued to say
"I got a B minus
On a very hard test.
Aren't you proud of me? You are.
Thank you, I love
You my good girl."
Repeating good girl, good girl, good girl, my good girl,
Front door slam,
Footsteps getting closer,
Her father, was home,
Stuttering footsteps,
Trips, falls to the floor
Breaking down to the floor,
Hardly getting back up
On his weary feet,
He takes a deep breath and slowly
Walks up to the top,

Steps getting closer,
One step at a time,
I had, some sort of feeling,
Even though I can't have them
I knew, she should not go out there,
No news of a B minus will save her
From drunken slurs and footsteps,
She ran out into the hall
And met eyes with him,
Always with a look so grim,
She showed him the test,
Her eyes, filled with joy,
The same she did
When she told me,
"Hey daddy, I got a good grade
On a very hard test,
I got a B minus,
See, are you proud of me?
Her father, did not speak
Just like me,
But he could,
His lips are not wax,
With red paint on them,
Heavy breathing, he looks down
At his joyful daughter,
I heard, another slam,
And the sound repeated,
Getting louder and louder,
Getting stronger and stronger,
Tears endless
All through the day,
And sleepless night,
She repeated, good girl, good girl, good girl, good girl,
I love you my good girl.

A Sobered Story

A middle aged, thin woman
Stands in front of an AA meeting,
Asking everyone, to welcome a man,
Onto the stage
That holds, a beach wood podium,
He comes up, speech written in one page,
Looks at it and crumbles it up
While shaking his head,
"I used to have a coffee cup"
he said,
"I drank my coffee, Irish
And sucked on vodka bottles, like a fish.
I have been sober for 200 days"
He pauses
As the crowd applauses
Filled with people
That need help, and see
Him as a possibility, that
There is a chance to become clean,
"200 days,
No more drinking by the bay,
One morning I woke up
With a screaming hang over,
My wife poured coffee into my cup
And she knew I had a problem,
She told me I hit my daughter,
Over and over again,
I can't remember what happened,
Well, I can't remember most of the night,
I remember coming home,
Barely coming climbing up the stairs,
Mouth watering, for the bottle of aspirin,

My daughter comes to me with a grin
Saying, hi daddy, hi,
Then she started to cry
As my hand made contact
Directly with her face,
The first time, I ever
Hit my little girl,
While the rest of the night is a blur
The hits, I remembered perfectly,
Over and over again,
I wish I could
Take that back,
Illusion of a smack
To my daughter's rosy cheeks,
A nightmare, that all,
But it, happened, bruises
To prove it,
I woke up that morning,
Wanting, to change my ways,
Sober for 200 days,
And counting,
200 days, my lips have not touched
A drop, of alcohol,
To tell you the truth,
I don't miss the memories around
The blurred nights,
Not a bit,
I don't sit
And wonder, if I made a mistake,
A habit, I had to break,
Or else, I would have lost
My love, my life, me,
It's a high cost
To get drunk night

After night
And even sinking into days,
Off that destructive poison,
On this, my 200th day,
I woke up
Without, my head throbbing
Without my clothes and eyes,
Smelling of alcohol,
I kissed my wife
And little girl,
I'm lucky that memory is a blur
In her mind,
Not in mine,
That was my low point
Where I just smacked
My sweet, little baby girl."
Tears from his eyes
Dropped, sinking into the stage,
Tears still continued to drop
As he pauses, the microphone pops,
"I will never, forgive myself,
Even though she does,
If I ever try, to take another drink,
Into a bottle of vodka, I'd want to sink,
Into a state of loneliness
I shall be,
I will loose,
Lost love, life, me,
All I have to do is think
Into memories, sink
Deep into it,
Past the blur,
And past the door
In a world

In a house
In a room,
I will never forgive myself
For hitting, my good girl."
Sobered story, taken off a lively shelf.

Water Over Dead

Does he lie in peace,
Does he roll, ever time he hears thunder,
The ground feels a tear from his only family, loving niece,
Touched six feet under,
The so called darkness, of his ways
Ridiculed by his faith, and teacher,
He spent his days,
As an innocent preacher,
What was so bad, about what he did,
About the way he wanted to live,
In his dream he hid
A romantic rose, what he wanted to give,
Lived his life, serving his belief
Never serving, himself,
Swept away the fallen leaf
And dusted, the spring dusty shelf,
His peers of faith, did not take him in,
Left to rot, outside,
For the "holy ground" can not touch sin,
My faith has died,
My arms, took him,
Took the "sinner" to his resting place ahead,
Washed away, when light was dim,
Washed away, water over dead.

Early Age Of War

I see the fear in his shaking eyes,
The struggle to hold in his cries,
Trying his best, to pick up his sword,
Scrawny, thin as a board
Taken to fight,
But he never lived a broken night,
Never had a broken heart
For his life did not even start,
His life can't fill up a worthy page
At this very early age,
Baby face
May see his resting place,
Taken to fight, for good,
Does not matter, to the gods of war,
That he will lie dead, on the floor,
As bone crushing feet will walk over him,
His eyes grow dim
As he continues to try,
To pick up his sword, he starts to cry,
No more can he hold in his tear,
He is overwhelmed by fear,
Pushed out to fight,
Swinging sword, ends the war night.

Enemy Of Faith

Did you ever wonder
What truth was thrown six feet under,
The good holy church bells chime
At each hour, of time,
Celebrating their deceit on the unknowing,
For their lies keep growing,
Truth hidden within a bell,
Evidence of truth fell
Into the hands, of a believer,
Now a griever,
Sympathy, in the death of his faith,
Once eyes meet the dark truth, of a wraith
Hidden, in the shadow,
Sent down to the inferno,
With those that sadly departed,
Believers, stand broken hearted.

Trapped In A Pocket Clock

Tick tock, tick tock
Goes the pocket clock,
Glance at the time
As the next hour, plays its chime,
Picture love in its keep,
Picture love, not when you sleep
But in the clock, in my pocket
Is the sweet romantic,
But, when opened, love is the first I see,
Love locks eyes with me,
And pulls my heart to her heart,
When did time start
Tick tock, tick tock,
Love trapped in the pocket clock,
Hopefully soon, free it shall run
Under the moon's sun,
Over the pain and hurt
Pushing aside, the heavy dirt
To break through, the hands of time,
In the next hours chime.

After Darkness

The eyes, of darkness laughs
At what the moon cries for,
The laughter of darkness echoes through,
As stars break through the dark cover
Bringing to light,
Now a translucent truth,
For after darkness
There is endless night,
Fighting for the moon and starry light.

Down goes a walking tree,
Pairs of eyes shocked, by what they see,
They are trapped in fear
And try not to drop a single tear,
It's a different walk
A different move,
For after darkness
There is endless night,
Fighting for the moon, and starry light.

Scared of their own name,
Scared of being seen in the same spot,
Fear of the dark flickering candle light
Fighting, for the moon and starry light,
The moon's light is never, the same
After darkness.

The Liveethiam House

Death politely knocks on the door
Only to find, suicidal deaths on the floor,
For eyes, see this in the shadow
Of a shady window,
The wife and daughter of Sir Liveethiam, lie dead
Eyes growing red,
The house up for sale
As the moon arrives, when the moon is pale,
"Welcome to the Liveethiam house" a man said
At the same time bowed his head,
"Please enter, come in."
He says with a devilish grin,
"The master of the house is floating around,
you might her him, if listen closely to his sound."
A strange silence comes over him,
As the room's lights grow dim,
"Follow me to you rooms, stay close to the candle."
He says grabbing the lighted handle.
"This is the dinning hall, where we shall be eating,
Oh, don't expect a welcome greeting,
Sir Liveethiam does not like others, buying his house
Taking a crumb of his life, like a mouse."
They get to their rooms within a single breath
Past the room of suicidal death,
"Don't get comfortable, dinner, shall be ready soon."
Now the only light source is the bright moon,
The white light tried to break through the heavy curtain,
The family is certain
This house is there's,
Coming down the poorly lighted stairs,
A ghostly reach is growing,
As covering clouds are flowing,

The bell rings
And the ghost sings,
The man says diner, is ready,
As the night air stays steady,
Through the eyes of fear
A spirit, drops like a tear
Off the cheeks of the pale moon,
" You shall join his wife and daughter soon."
Another sale, had to die
As Sir Liveethiam awaits another drive by,
Another family to show, this house is not for sale,
For the night, shall always show the moon, pale.

Hibernation Of A Mind

I thought I was a normal kid,
Played with my friends, I did,
Went to school and did my homework,
But inside, something lurked
Something in my mind
And I went blind,
Not only in my eyes, my whole body dies,
Seemed like I fell asleep
Didn't snore, didn't say a peep,
My eyes, were still open, but I didn't see
Didn't know what was happening to me,
Inside of me, everything was alive
But it seemed, my mind did not survive,
Couldn't move around
Or even make a sound,
Mentally I was dead
Nothing was happening in my head,
One day I awoke from dream,
In a white hall, heaven it would seem,
I looked around
And saw other people, who were bound
To a bed, or a chair,
And they would just sit and stare
Not at anything specific,
For all I knew, they were looking at a still Pacific,
At the end of the hall
There was a window, on the wall
As I got closer, an image would appear,
I am in fear
For the 45 old image, mimics me,
A 15 old mind is me.

Bound To That Star

I look up at the night sky
And find its first star,
I am bound, to its glow
Even when hidden, behind the clouds flow
I am, bound to that star.

If another star shall appear
My desire will not disappear
For, my blue yes can't wait for night,
When I will be able to see the star,
For I am bound, to that star.

If a bright star comes out,
And others say, it's bigger,
My heart is bound
To that star, and not the others around,
For my heart is bound, to that star.

All around the pale moon's eyes
I see, twinkling stars in the night's sky,
I look at the starry night
To find out my star, is not in sight,
Fear comes to my bounded heart.

In the midnight hour
I see my starry flower
Looking into the eyes, from the sand,
Reached out for her hand,
I am bound to that star
In the starry sky.

Street Sweeper

Six in the morn
Before men hear, that waking horn,
Before the sun reaches its highest peak of heat,
He is out on the street,
Sweeping the garbage, of the fast pace walkers,
And ignorant talkers,
Not only garbage, but tears,
And overwhelming fears
Litter the streets of the city,
It is he, who makes it clean and pretty,
Until the raging bulls are on the run
After the pale moon sun,
Finishing their coffee to the floor
Exit through the park door,
The street sweeper is there
With eyes, open in stare
To the shock of dirt, on the street
Sinking feet,
Slowly growing deeper
Is the street sweeper,
He takes out his broom, begins to sweep
While others, still sleep,
It takes him from day to night,
Where no garbage is in sight,
Aching feet of the street sweeper
Followed by aching eyes, of the light sleeper,
Does anyone care to know his name
Does anyone care, that he stays inside the frame
Of the city's dirt
And it's professional shirt,
His child's words, run cold
As his tears are on hold.

"Sorry these eyes have been disconnected,
But my heart has been affected
For I see his eyes, when he comes to mine,
Telling myself, he's fine,
I am loved by my wife and son
But telling lies are done,
I only show the truth, never do I lie
For finally tears fall, from a cry,
Its time my eyes close
And I lay in a rested pose."
It has all caught up with him
For the morning light, will always stay dim.

Time Lost In A Story

Can you,
Would you, count the hours in a book
That contains a story,
Told passionately
With the desire and interest
That his love will remain,
Can time be counted
Would time be sought out,
Trying to see
And find out
How much longer, do I have to read,
Time is lost in a story
About guts and glory
About the passionate hate,
The love that lives, after death,
Bring on the romantics
To talk of the nightly fog
Where shrieks are heard,
The love you are not allowed to have,
My friends, my people,
Brothers, sisters,
My mother and father
Should know that I
Am a story teller,
And all are lost
Within my passionate words.

Hooded Head

Characterized by appearance,
What's wrong with the way I look,
I walk up to the up class
As the rich folks stare
In disgust,
In a way that makes you feel
That you are the lowest dirt,
The piece of meat stuck in their rich teeth
Let's see, they work for a living,
Not that high corporate desk
Who lies and cheats,
They deserve it in return.

Walk into the middle class
And strange looks, still come along,
Parents pulling their child
"Come on, he's nasty and dirty"
Kids feel differently.

I am in Manhattan,
Just one of the bums
But do me a small favor now,
Look under my hooded head,
My eyes say different,
Am I really what you think.

The Shadowed Reflection

I look at my reflection
Cast, by the glaring sun,
You can't see my hideous face
And unpleasant features,
My acne corroded face
And plank sized nose,
The disturbing features
That are too hideous to look at,
In a real reflection, perhaps a mirror
No, it might break
Seriously, I don't joke,
Ten of them already broke
For I just stand there, and it shatters,
The image I am scared to look at,
I'm fat
I'm ugly
My ears stick out,
So does my nose,
Do you really want me, to strike a pose,
Vogue, GQ, or the cover of any magazine,
All my blubber would shake
As the water moves, as I step, look at the lake,
Jurassic Park all over again,
The fish jump away,
I go out at night, stay gone from day,
The shadowed reflection is friendlier
To me, at least.

I'm older now
I've changed, how
I lost weight,
And grew into my looks,

I stay out of the shadow
And in at times,
But not to hide myself,
I am comfortable with my self
For I am a different hear
Mind, face, and body,
The ugly duckling effect.

Love After The Grave

Family portrait set over the fireplace,
Frozen memories of a, young face,
Father, mother, and child,
The mother's hair, is styled,
The father, fresh shave
And the child is smiling, a memory to save,
A mere picture is all that remains,
A smile stands out, when it rains,
A love alive after death
Stolen, is the baby's breath,
Stolen, was the love they, couldn't let go
Stolen, from the river's flow,
Memories stay frozen
Love forever stolen,
Memories stolen, in a stare,
But love, will always be there.

An Orphan's Tale

I see the night air from the ground below,
I see the world in a saddened flow,
There I am on a cold sidewalk, in New York
For I could have been brought by a stork,
All there was, was a child empty of a mother's bearing
And a father's caring,
Arms, find my cold abandoned eyes
Funny that I shed no cries,
This is what, I was told
Truth to heavy to hold,
I found myself reading to silence
Listening to my own words getting tense,
I was a newborn when I was found
Left on a sidewalk, now making that tearful sound,
A piece of loose leaf paper was clipped to my shirt,
I was left in New York dirt
To be found by anyone who cared
Anyone who dared
To pick up a screaming baby,
A church found me, anyone else would be crazy,
They brought me in
And hoped for a grin
From this baby that was left with a key and a note,
Some say, I was left by a black coat
And the rest of that person is me
The black coat roams free,
A strange man, came by once to check
The baby, see if I was his, placed the key around my neck,
A peculiar day, the man took off
Never to be seen again, disappeared in a cough,
Tears of the sky run down
The tall dark buildings of the city's crown,

I am at the age of four,
A couple walks through the orphanage door,
They're looking to adopt a child,
One that is not so wild,
They look through the pictures of orphan kids,
Place them down, what are your bids,
They come across one young boy
Thinking he can give them tons of joy,
Papers are signed to give me away
On this cold, and rainy day,
Step after step into a new scene
As they introduce me, to their daughter, a young teen,
She had blonde hair
And the colors of her eyes, were rare,
Blue and green eyes, un-welcomed me
To other, her look was too dim to see,
Hiding behind the stage light
Is her feelings within the night,
But my eyes break through
The darkened clouds, into the night sky, true,
A the father's lips hug the mouth of a drink,
The father's arms hug the body of pink,
For my eyes saw this, the weeks I was there,
My covered head would stare,
At the moments when pink was not around
I would feel the drunken sound,
Back to the orphanage after the bruised eye,
Didn't shed a cry
When I left the house of pain
On a day filled with rain,
Grim days follow
As passing nights get harder to swallow,
I sit on my assigned bed, feeling empty
Of a loving family

Looking through a magazine
Seeing different families, in a scene
As a very young couple, walks in through the orphanage door,
I see a picture of a family by the shore,
They saw me from afar
And minutes later, they're loading my bags into their car,
No daughter, no son
Except for the adopted one,
The husband is never around,
Lonely nights have her tearful sound,
Covered by her lies
Only seen in her eyes
Are her sad feelings so true,
For her heart wears the black and blue,
She starts to smile, as she likes to hang out with me
And talks of her faint memory
Of a mother and father, she was so nice
To my heart, taking it off that block of ice
And filling life with a loving family
She is like a sister to me,
Finally daylight breaks in,
The faint sign of a grin
Scene on the face of the moon,
Seen in a Saturday morning cartoon,
The link to darkness is lost in light
But comes back, with a fight,
My connection to the darkened tear
Disrupted by the one we fear,
She is now scared to talk
Scared of the painful walk,
The next day I awake from sleep
I don't hear that disturbing peep,
Walk into her bedroom and see her eyes flicker,
Her open eyes are a mere sticker

That hides her darkened tear
And unwanted fear,
She found me by her bed
Good morning was not even said
As she got up, and locked herself in the bathroom,
The morning had an eerie gloom
Nothing seemed right
Not even that bright glaring sunlight,
Three hours pass
Cold tears, lie in a glass,
Back to the orphanage after the darkened tear departed
As I sit broken hearted,
Brought upon my closed eyes
Are images that brought forth cries,
The darkened tear, lies still
Under the power of his thrill,
The moon of the house sees me for one night
As I am adopted to the dim light,
Dead to the outside
But within the comfort of her bed, where she loves to hide,
My new caretaker had a familiar look,
Blue and green read on the cover of a book
For pink rose up to go back down
For her mind, sits in frown,
No words were exchanged between our heavy breath,
Her actions reminded life of death
And her eyes reminded the light
Of the tall hand of night,
Did she remember me from the house of pain,
A house that drove her insane,
I sat fearing, she did,
When I was just a little kid
She gave me a look so grim
For back then, her face was dim,

And still, her face stay the same,
It was me that she wanted to blame
Like before me, everything was normal
And life was formal,
Laughs up and down
The growth of age
On and off the stage,
I sat and feared her reason
For all year is her insanity season,
Why did she adopt me
I would have to wait and see,
Streets started throwing memories
Familiar streets, signs, and trees
And there it was,
It was like time had been put on pause
The house of pain, was in sight
The darkness in the light
Was the house,
Where the giant hurt the hiding mouse,
I couldn't stand the silence anymore
I asked her, what she adopted me for
Why she took me in,
She turned to me with a grin.
She said, "You helped me
You might not see
That you did
But a little kid
Jailed my abusive father, my rapist,
I enjoy living ins the Sunkist
Of a mind described as insane,
But I am finally out of the house of pain."
She took me back
As the sun lasted through a crack,
Today is my eighteenth birthday

And I made it through a long way
As I wake up from the smell of a candle in flame,
Wake up from a dream of blame,
Woken by the sound of a song
I did no wrong,
The candles were blown out
Walk free, just about,
The priest that found me on the street
Eighteen years ago, asked me to take a seat.
"I'm sorry we couldn't get you a stable family
And instead placed, an awful memory
Into your overloaded head,
Couldn't even provide you with a better bed."
He handed me an envelope with my name,
"I feel shame
That I couldn't have done any better
When I found you with this letter,
I kept this note for you, for eighteen years
As it was all covered in your tears
Soaked, I took you in and I cared
For you, like you were my own, I never barred
To see you be taken, but I did try to find
A family for you, but my mind
And heart, hoped you would consider, us as a family
The little girls, boys, nuns, and me."
He got up hugged my heart grown
And left me alone,
Nothing but silence as I stared
For I dared
Myself to read,
My hands would lead
And my eyes followed
Into a world hollowed
By the opening line.

"I am your birth father, you were mine"
My heart dropped and squeezed in my small toe
As it continued, "I had to let you go
For my girlfriend, your mom had died,
She had lied
To this devil
As she sunk to his level
And used his lies against him,
Here eyes were in yours, but yours were more dim
Not as bright,
Yours were closer to the night,
I was scared, I needed to run
Towards the moon, not the sun."
That was it,
Within one paragraph, it all fit,
Except for an address on the bottom line in bold,
This piece I would hold
As I arrived, it was an apartment, a room
For it stayed within this eerie gloom,
I entered with a key I always had
Given to me, the lad,
That strange man that saw me
And gave it a new memory,
I opened up and saw a picture of my family,
Me, my father, mother
And another,
The darkened tear
The one that sadly had to disappear,
My loving family
In a picture, with me.

Extremity Of My Love

Countless ways,
Immeasurable ways,
I love you breaking words of expression
Through the walls of love's impression,
I love you to any depth and any height
For my love breaks free from the shadow, of the night,
I love you with a passion, I knew nothing about
For with a shout,
I tell you of my love
From down below, or up above,
I confess the birth of my love
For before you, love was unheard of,
Now I'm lost within your eyes
For I hear no cries,
With every breath, blink, and tear
I love you, without any fear,
Here is my love's expression
In my love's confession.

The Forbidden Leaves

Deep within the heart of a forest
Is a leaf-full tree
Surrounded by the leafless trees,
Leaves stay green throughout all four seasons,
They do not turn yellow,
Only can they turn white
During a winter night,
Forbidden, are those living leaves,
Not even a step is allowed
Around the reaches of its roots,
The mystic legend is heard through out
Spoken by the mouth of the forest in a shout
For the story, to be heard
The forest is scared to be ignored
By the ears of the destroyers of nature,
A long time ago,
A long time from any day this story was told
Where nature ruled over life,
A storm brewed over this certain tree
And it started to rain,
Sounds of an angry sky started,
The lightning darted
Striking the head of the tree,
Incinerating the core,
Giving the life of the tree
To the leaves,
The power of nature lives
Within each leaf,
Forbidden to touch, take, and pick,
The leaves contain mystic powers
Never dropping in the fall,
Never feeling the freezing winter,

Never springing in spring,
Always alive in summer,
Always alive,
No matter what force
Comes to harm.

Sisterhood

They care for one another
They truly care for each other,
One lives to be taken by men,
Been up and around since she was only ten,
She had a beautiful and happy look
Only on the cover of the book,
Inside was a different story to be told,
A story not to hold
Inside was truth of her emotion
And her devotion,
To sisterhood, a sisterhood the other couldn't deny
That she was apart of, oh she would try,
But no one believed her word,
For some never heard
Her speak,
They described her voice as meek,
She wasn't seen to often,
Sometimes one would ask, if she lies in her coffin
Ready to be sent to the heavenly lord,
She is the half that looked through a sword
Contemplating death
Admiring her last breath
And then, the other half would come in,
Stopping her of that sin
Just in the nick of time,
The sisterhood are both criminal and victim in a crime,
They both shared the same name,
One played game
The other stayed in the rain
Which do you define as sane?

Rough Winds

Rough winds chill my heart,
Rough winds go round, and about
Touching my whole, touching every part,
I despise the howling shout.

As I lie in a crowd of fallen leaves, I find
I am taken by the rough winds that chill,
An entry that, just came to my mind,
I am taken, for I lie still.

An Ode Of Death

Power lies within this heart
Power spilled within this cart
Define the meaning of death
Define why she has no more breath
The power and rage of one
Destroys a life, a life that is done
Hunt for a kill, which is done for pleasure,
That is power's measure,
To strike a body dead, to the coldest touch,
Is what he loves to do way too much,
Death in the hands of man
Death done, because he can,
Winter is a friend to the murdering crime
For darkness, conquers time.

Snow Surrounded Cabin

I need to escape from everyday pressure
The stress
That presses me down
That pushes me down
That flattens me, not my frown,
To run away from the one
With the devil-sided crown
Exiled from the tortures rule
And side help fool,
I need to escape
From the everyday goblins
Young and old
I need to fold
For I bluff without even a pair,
Uh oh, a gray hair,
And I'm only twenty
Isn't that funny,
Deep in the snow covered forest
Sits a cabin
That I can safely, without stress, stay in,
Surrounded by snow
Surrounded by a white glow,
Hidden from those that yell
And talk like they are as loud, as a church bell,
My heart feels lighter
Stress free, all nighter
And through out the day,
Escaped from the tight grasp
Of the low balled rule,
I have to run out from the open
Into the snowy shadow
In the cabin,

By the fireplace,
For here, life is no race
To finish, to complete, to get done
So I can punch out from stress,
But still follows like the storm cloud
Over my head, rain
And thunder stay, hovering
My already clouded mind,
No rule,
Of a fools
"creative and fair" make,
Pleasure is mine to take
Looking out into the frozen lake
Under the white clouds
That lie in front of the night sky
Letting in the snow covered moon,
For I find this all
Deep behind the snow covered trees
Snow covered fallen leaves,
To the snow covered roses,
I stay within the comfort
Of the snow surrounded cabin.

Student In Shadow

I walk amongst the normal, the sane,
And off-course the insane,
I go from class to class
Lesson to lesson, hoping I can pass,
While the normal, sane, and insane are in sunlight,
I am in the cold and windy shadow,
My feet take me to a house
At the bottom of a hill,
Enter, words are exchanged
I leave with a card in my right jacket pocket,
Still images of memories
And dream images
Take my mind into its control,
They swallow me whole
An end to breath
Seen from my eyes,
She cries, he cries, a flood of tears,
For me? No
Life still has its flow
Even though
My heart and mind are in shadow,
What it is, I ask,
Nobody around to answer
Nobody can give me reason
The right way to think it,
My right jacket pocket
An appointment at nine in the morning,
Do I stay in the deep shadow
Or slowly come out
Giving my mind ease,
Relief from those images
Will it come

Or will images come fierce,
Destroying any trace
Of a smile, happiness, and love,
I don't want that to leave
Don't want it to go,
For if necessary I'll run out
Into the rain, and shout
Just, scream to release my heart
From the dream,
I can't run out from the shadow
For it follows
Me where ever I turn
Where ever I sleep,
Dreams find my heart
In every step,
The shadow's eyes stick to me
And never leave me,
I can't concentrate on what has to be done,
For my mind is haunted
While trapped in darkness of a shadow,
Where to go, for house
At the bottom of the hill
Can't help me,
For it can't see
Inside my head
That has an abundance of dead
Still images, those are my dreams,
Am I one of the dead images,
Yes.

Alas A Sight

A girl blind from the beauty's scene since
The day of her birth,
Never has she seen the colors of the sunset,
Never has she seen the clear blue sky,
Instead she has been behind the gray clouds,
Love for her is truly blind,
She walks about the whole world shadowed
The whole world covered by darkness,
A voice, a step, a simple smell
Who it is, she can tell.

Her step is not as firm
Not as strong, or sure,
She leaves her eyes on the nightstand
Not really needing them to go about,
Yet she has the weaker step,
A tear drops to her hand
She can barely stand
On her own two feet
The night,
The loss, the never having of sight
Breaks her down to an incomplete,
She stands, tries to be discrete
Unnoticeable to any eye
Not noticing, she wants to cry,
Giving the lamppost a hug.

Day, the celebration of her birth
The oohs and ahhs of extravagant gifts,
Her spirit never lifts,
Never does she smile
From excitement or from a joke,

Strait face through,
Go on, blow out your candles,
"Where are they?"
The cake, right in front of her,
Her sight is not even a blur, but complete darkness,
She blows, everyone claps and cheers
As a spirit is lifted, she smells the smoke
As everyone continued to blow.

Night comes for her twenty four, seven,
It is time for her, to sleep,
She feels it is that time
As she kneels beside her bed.

"Enter Happiness,
Enter life,
Enter one and all, the sights of strife,
End to darkness,
End to pitch black,
Alas a sight,
No more night.

When My Rose Was Gone

To my red, red rose
Whose warmth I miss during the winter chill,
I count the days till you bloom
Till then I pray the cruel wind still,
I need to know when you'll return,
When you'll once again be in sight,
I wait for you,
Wait for the romantic night.

When my rose was gone
Foolish was I, look up at the pale sun,
Then back down at the bed,
The flower that slept was not red,
A flower whose name must not be spoken
To my rose, a petal found, her bud would be broken,
The flower was Tiger Lilly, a tiger indeed,
Even furious as a seed,
The rose owns my heart
Each and every part,
For when my rose was gone, my heart, my heart lost,
Now I'm stuck in the winter frost.

In Between Raindrops

Can you see through the pouring rain,
Which drop, does it contain
Secrets, can your eyes tell
Or are they under a deep darkened spell,
Differentiate a drop of winter from spring,
Which song do the rain drops sing?
Which song indeed
A storm rumbles in the seed
Of a cloud, one so gray, its color is mistaken
For a color of the forsaken,
Can you see in between the raindrops of a storm,
In between raindrops of a swarm,
The reason for drops that fall,
I see it when they stall,
For my clear blue eyes breaks in
And commits the secret sin,
I found which raindrop contains
Secrets, running to the drains.

Door

Lights on and off,
Door leads me up and down,
Whether I want to be in the, comfort
Of the outside
Or the chaotic world, of the in,
Judged and put down
As soon as I walk in through the door,
The door could lead me out into
My carpeted floor
And wallpapered walls,
In one room, three stage lights are on
Pointed at the center,
Smile, could I, would I
Enter or turn to the door
That leads me in to the outside,
Where more hands help, and skies clear
Even if drops fall,
I'm stuck in the middle of the hall,
Two doors on opposite sides
And I need the chaotic,
So I can rest, sleep, but
Not peacefully, unfortunate
For that door, I rather look
To the outside, where respect
And love was found
And will always be around
For sure, not doubting that thought,
Not making second choices, or last minute
Decision, in or out
I rather be out, turn to the door
To lead me up,
Let my words echo

Outside, for they are always ignored
When yelled in,
Ask the door, leave me out
Lock once or lock twice,
Throw away the key to let
My heart and mind
Let it
Be. Disrupted.

Flow Of Art

Come here and rest
Your head upon my chest
And listen to my poetic heart,
Listen to the beauty, the flow of art,
Now feel my heart beat out words in poetic flow
A story of the midnight glow,
Blood flows into the babbling brook of my heart
And into the river's flow of art,
Let your ears listen to the sunset
And the colors caught resting in the water's net,
Now tell me, what do you hear?
For the flow of art, brings you a tear.

Murderous Crime

A mind sits alone,
It ponders all day and night
Of what it can and can not do,
Thoughts enter and leave
For some enter and stay,
Disturbing, they are,
They pollute the mind
And demand to be thrown into motion,
Off-course some minds would leave it in the ocean
Of flowing thoughts,
But there lives a mind
Who longs for those thoughts
To be, physically reachable,
The river of light
Rolls clouds, turning day to night,
Turning that mind wild,
A surrealistic night of craze,
Of thoughts go into action
Striking one after another cold,
Chill, still, the mind can do more
Than kill a moment in time,
It can strike winter
Into the warmest of hearts,
The mind goes on a rampage,
Lifting the heart of the inferno
Into the power of the mind's
Tortures, and death filled hands,
A black rose, rose of the murderous one
Laid upon his cold eyes
Of, frightful eyes,
Can't be caught
For death lives only in thought,

Day returns, realistic,
The mind stays within thought
Until that moment, where darkness
Shines through the clouds,
The striking hand,
Completes the vision, that laid dormant
In the mind, till a word,
Event, sight, brought out the darkness,
But for now
In the loneliness of a mind,
There is no murderous crime
For it just sits in the mind
That sits alone,
For now, it only ponders all day and night,
The murderous mind can
And will live, in the body
Of one that sees darkness, in his very own eyes.

Wintered Lake

The moon is reflected
In the still eyes of the lake that is connected
All in one frozen piece,
The lake wears its icy fleece,
The winter has chilled the body,
The winter has custody
Of the coldest touch brought to mind,
Warmth, the one thing the lake can never find
Never felt, for all year round
Frozen to the very ground,
The winter makes
Frozen tears, lie still in its eyes
And frozen are those cries,
Even though they are chilled, they are heard
Even though they don't stream down, they are heard,
Winter storm arrives on the lake
On the frozen body, never wake,
For years the lake has slept,
And its chipped icy heart, swept
Out of its reach, gone to sleep
For years in the winter's keep,
Where is the warmth, the dawn of summer
Spring, fall, and winter,
To protect it from the cold splinter,
Its eyes stay shut, and cold,
Hoping one day, warmth to hold,
Can you see it in the moon
That warmth is coming soon,
Heard through the winter snow
Look through the lake's frozen window,
Go along the snowy trail
Walk past through the falling hail

And find its frozen heart,
Frozen, but not in one part,
The single beat
Touched by the summer's heat,
The birth of seasons gives a kiss
For warmth is felt in her lips, the bliss
Of summer's hear, the lake is a flow
For it still reflects the moon's glow.

Darkened Days

Shadows creep out
From the deepest darkness,
Even the candle lights are blown out
By the howling wind of the darkened days,
Every crack is filled by the night
Every light
Stays in its darkened shadow,
Day is taken over by
The power of the night,
The call, for the shadow
To fall onto the moon
Covering the glow of light,
Not a single light is seen
By mine, or any pair of confused eyes,
Where is the day
When the sun gave us vision,
When the moon showed us the way,
How far to the next sun
For I will count to that day
That turns night
Into the clearest light,
Darkened days fall onto us
Fall onto the lights flickering
In the sunset,
A sun that sets to sleep
And to close its eyes
Till the day of peace,
To show us light
When darkness fails to reach
Its point, its reason, its idiotic lessons,
Darkened days arrive carrying
A bag full, of fear, of despair, and of death,

It sits in the comfort of that bag,
As war breaks out and into
My heart, filled already with
Sadness, for I sit and await
The sun's lighted step,
Weapons of war dropped on my porch,
They ask of my help,
Of my heart to sink
Into the arms of the darkened days,
When the rule to fight
Is composed, I fear it
When the words to kill
Is composed, I fear all
That lives to fight for fear,
I fear the living
And fear for the dead,
For my fingers to touch a weapon of death
Is to sell
What is not mine to sell
In the first place, my soul,
Who am I to bring others death,
Who do darkened days call upon me,
To act for it, put my body in motion
And fight till
There is no more darkness,
I fear, darkness will never end,
No light shall be seen,
No sunrise
At the top of the mountain,
It will not come into the
Sight of my yes
And my heart,
I will not bring myself
Into doing what I

Can not do in the first place,
I am not a taker of life,
War falls upon the world
And all are suppose to fight
For the land that we live in,
That they love, darkened days
Come and go,
How long they stay, is up to
The way we live them.

Eyes Falling To Shadow

A family gathers at a time of grief,
At a time, when a tree looses its leaf,
A child sneaks away to a room
Where you can see the flower's bloom,
The boy enters and finds a man in his deathbed,
A man whose life, could not be left unsaid
To the boy's young mind,
A life ready to rewind
To the very beginning of his eyesight,
Born on a star filled night,
From that first day
His eyes were the brightest, already on their way
To find, achieve the sight beauty
In a world that sits without majesty,
At the age of thirteen he decides how to reach
How to teach
Young minds, a story ready to be told,
A star filled night when the air is cold,
Birth given to a boy,
A boy later on, all wanted to destroy,
Born into royalty in a flowerless land
For it is covered in stone, gravel, and sand,
Seemed like his home was destined to be in ruble
For the palace nested in trouble,
Rulers from neighboring courts looked down
On the boy's father, the one that wears the crown,
At the age of four
War had broken outside the palace door
As well as inside,
Both wars had started from the towering pride
Of the boy's father, death stabbed
Into the king, into the boy, pain was jabbed

Not really knowing he lost his father, death
Was unknown, breadth
Of passing was very small
For the boy knew nothing of dying, nothing at all,
Being too young to rule,
They appointed a cardinal, not exactly a fool
Still, he appeared so slippery, trust, slipped through
The fingers of the boy, he knew what was true
About the cardinal, he was despised
By the far reaches, past were the sun rised
To bring light upon any land,
The boy's home lied un-restful in the cardinal's hand,
The war has stopped with the death of the king,
With the passing down of the family ring
To a young finger, too young to rule
And a mother that died, a world so cruel,
The boy stood alone in shadow
As time went on, sadness would only grow,
In his heart sat pain
Sat a grain
Of happiness with the spirit of his pen
Finding beautiful words stuck in a den
And his mind, was setting them free
For all to hear and see
Onto the paper living, in books,
For all who can, to read of the crooks,
Taking lives into their hands, and crushing
Them into little pieces, from land to land flushing
Out those who oppose the new rule,
He showed all the people the pool
Of lies they all were swimming in,
He showed their grin
At the bottom, water of despair
Over the heart of the heir

To the kingdom, destined to die in shadow
Light never to show
Upon the heart of the land in ruin,
The bad ways, the sin
Of the kingdom, breaking, destroying peace,
The boy wrote,
Recorded and revised into a story, not
The first piece of literature from the boy's
Bright eyes, for war's toys
Were used against his heart,
Killing his father and tearing his mother apart,
The boy's words were putting ideas of life,
One without strife,
A beautiful palace covered by nature
And love to nurture,
The cardinal despised his words of liberation,
He hated this literary creation,
A war broke loose,
The boy, did not want a truce
For he still had not trust to give
No trust would live
In the cardinal's hand,
The boy was ready to take the land
And put it in better shape, into beauty,
Instead of a far off memory
It would be seen, if he could get the rule,
The cardinal wanted war for spilling lies out of the pool,
All the boy had was words in his book
About the crook,
Cardinal, it was up to the boy's pen
To break in to the lion's den
And destroy the corrupt rule
Of an unforeseen fool,
"The Book Of Demons" was written to destroy

the cardinal by the boy,
all the secrets of his rule and mind
were released to all the blind,
Poetic Heart killed the cardinal's way
And put an end to the rule in the mid summer's day,
In a life committed to the written word,
It is what the boy saw and heard
That put the kingdom at rest,
The boy restored the world's family crest,
Majesty in art, he lives in the glow
Of the majestic moon, as well as the star's flow.

Threads

The threads of a heart
Can be broken by a shattered mirror,
Once a whole threaded heart
It has been pulled on
By the thorns of roses,
For each thread of that heart
Is still caught in the thorn full stem,
Pieces of thread lays a path
To where the remainder of the
Heart lie, under the shadow
Of the harvest moon,
Ten million pairs of eyes look
Past the heart, incomplete it sits,
Broken it walks its path,
The threads of a heart blow
Within the cold winter wind,
Pain is the color
Of the torn apart
Low threaded heart,
A throne of past thorns
Haunts this heart's, every dream
And waking moment,
Pointed thorns of cold touches
Clutches
The rest of me,
The rest of what can be,
A healed, and mended heart.

The threads of a mind
Can be influenced by harsh words,
It has been picked at
So others can learn

And take away its power
For these words, words that
Are being read, is the power
The mind possesses and
Can never let go,
The threads let go,
The threads are being cut
By the knives
Of the fairy tale lives,
The mind says goodnight
To that tale
And hello, to the reality
Of true life, to threads of the mind,
A sight gone blind
From the intake of harsh words.

Threads of a body
Can be hurt by the high temperature fire,
For within the flick of a match,
Those threads can easily burn
Easily does the body yearn
To be held
In loving arms within the night,
As easy as it yearns
It hurts when those threads
Feel the unkindly and unloving
Touch, of the blistering fire,
The six piece puzzle
Sits on the table,
Put together by the threads
Of the only lonely
Thread of me.

The threads of me
Can be broken, influenced, and hurt
By the legend, and mystery
Known as the night,
Only can the threads be
Touched if I allow it,
I put the puzzle together
With six elements of what makes,
What made me become
The man I am,
The threads of me
Are safe without a hurtful broken memory
Under the soft flower tree.

Battle Between Two Dragon Hearts

A crystal gem rose
Sits in the dark echoed heart
Of a cave, protected by a fire
Breathing dragon, without wings,
It walks through the mystic
Forest of the land,
Another dragon heart desires
The possession of the gem rose,
A war has been raging on
For as long as I can recall,
Two fierce hearts battle
For the mystic beauty
That lies within the crystal gem rose,
The hypnotic beauty of the rose can
Take over any heart it comes
In contact with,
Many believed it was false, a myth,
But as the war raged on
A battle came out from the forest
Onto a kingdom,
A knight found the rose in the cave,
Wondering lost in the forest
He found the cave, and found its rose,
Stumbled upon its beauty and power,
The knight snatched it and ran off
Out of the forest,
The protector was battling the other dragon
In the high peaks of the mountain,
Both dragon hearts sensed its capture,
Its lost eyes and heart,
Simultaneously the two dragons
Appeared, one in the sly flapping its

Long span wings, the other
At the gate door,
All the people of the kingdom ran
To where they could be safe,
The kingdom was a ghostly town
Except for the mystic beauty
That rested in the tower,
The gate door was torched by the dragon
Stomping on anything and everything,
Smashing structures of the kingdom,
The other dragon flew the tope,
Finally the rose
Came into the sights of both
Fierce hearts,
Under the moon shade
These two hearts battled
For the beauty of the crystal gem rose,
Still the war rages on
For the rose never sits in the possession
Of one dragon, for too long,
The two fierce hearts, will always battle
Till one dies, and the rose
Becomes the heart of that dragon,
To have beauty, not fiery fierceness,
In their heart.

Shower Stall

Shower drops beat off
Her tear soaked body,
As she sits in the shower stall
Counting her tears that mix in
With the shower tears,
She prays in her tear drowned voice,
That an answer to her struggle
And tortures pain
Will come along soon,
Her eyes open to the past,
A life that wouldn't, that couldn't last,
Her pale eyes stay in a blank state
As her mouth drops open,
Catching the tears of the moon,
The shower stall continues to throw tears,
All around her head are fears,
The memories, her strain
Within the night's, shower rain,
No more,
Lock and unlock the shower door.

Discussion Group

A circle is formed by seven chairs
In a room filled with vague stairs,
This room also contains secrets
Shared by six people, secrets
That linger n the six chairs, secrets
That weighs down the seventh chair,
A room filled with concern and care,
One by one, by one, their stories are told,
Stories that will haunt the seventh chair till he dies of old,
Aged in his heart
It becomes stronger, it becomes apart
Of the seventh pair of eyes,
The seven stories ties
Together, but in the end
Each will fade, never to blend
In within the snowy weather
Of the floating feather,
Fade away back to the past,
The beginning, when happiness had a chance to last,
Those seven stories began
Simultaneously with the start of the flower's growth span,
Then one, by one, by one, secrets are set free
Into the room, dark and haunting memory
Comes out of each chair, one by one,
Eyes and hearts open wide, "are you done?",
Not nearly, the end is far, at least for him
Six chairs grow dim,
The seventh stays in its seat
Feeling the spotlight's glowing heat,
Fade away the first and second,
Tick tock of a second
And there goes the third,

Life is stirred
And there goes the fourth, fifth, and last,
Six friends are a thing of the past.

The Lost Legend

Frozen in the snow is a legend's words
Lost to the ears, a tale never heard,
Only one knows of the story,
Only one knows of its memory,
The lost legend sank
To the bottom of the snowing bank,
Where no heart hears of it,
It becomes the snow river's secret,
Only one heart remains
That knows, what the story contains,
Only that heart knows
Why the story flows
In the frozen river, kept silent,
Kept still, and content
Are the ears and hearts,
That lie dreaming the story's different parts,
For deep down, if a heart hasn't heard
The lost legend's words,
There is the only heart that lives
To tell, a lost legend to give
For as long as he is around,
A lost legend to be found
Within the melting snow
Of the snowy river's flow,
Death comes to the heart
Who tells the legend, he departs,
Sadly with the legend of him,
His own heart and tale dies grim,
Words never to reach another ear,
A legend forever lost, the heart's greatest fear.

Plead

Candlelit diner for two
Under the moon of blue,
She sits alone waiting for her love
To show, she waits looking at the stars above,
A second that turns to a minute, an hour goes by
As she starts to wonder why
He still isn't there,
Empty sits the chair
As she begins a stream
Of tears, that night a dream
Of her love that disappears
Into the sky, awake with overwhelming fears,
A ring of the phone,
She picks up with a tearful tone,
It was her love apologizing
For not being there way before the rising
Of the morning sun, her tears started to stream down
To the sides of her frown,
She hung up the phone without a word
Before a single cry was heard,
She had nothing to say
No voice to use, clouds of gray
Pass by her eyes of blue,
She sat wondering where he was and with who,
Her mind could only think of the worst,
Off-course cheating was the first
Reason that came up, and would not leave,
Her mind, floated into a tight fitted sleeve
That gave her no room for breath, caught
In the darker territory, she sought
Out for worst reason of a lasting splinter
In the rose, which kills the flower in the winter,

The phone rings, she knows it's him,
It doesn't stop as the sun grows dim
It doesn't stop as the moon is its brightest,
The sleeve is at its tightest
As her love comes to her window
And pleading under the moon's glow,
But he could not find light of her,
The winter weather was in a stir
As the could of gray bring frozen rain, that surrounds
The pleading sounds,
The subtle sound sitting in his throat,
A winter rose pulled from his coat,
Winter flakes cover the rose's crown,
As her tears stream down
He finds her in the moonlight
Imbedded in the starry night.

Letter To Heart

As the moon gives the house
Its only light, the lock turns open,
Heart calls out for her,
Calls out her name
As it echoes into the dark,
He finds it strange, that the house
Is without her being,
Flick, the light brightens the room,
He continues from room to hall, to room,
Turning darkness brighter,
Upstairs to downstairs,
Heart erases the shadows from the chairs,
Winter frost on the eyes of the house
Bringing frozen tears,
He walks into the last room
Where darkness still lingers,
Light brings attention to an envelope
With "Heart" written on it,
He starts to think it's finally over,
That she did what he dreamt
What he saw in his mind
And what he felt deep within
His heart, happened,
From the way she smiled
To the way she walked into a room,
Darkness, would be better
Than the light upstairs and downstairs,
Better to have the shadow
On those same empty chairs,
As he walks closer to heartbreak,
He can't help it, he drops a frozen
Tear of sadness, he pick up the letter

As the door opens,
And there she was,
Standing in the doorway,
She saw his tears and asked
What was wrong,
He asked where she was
Clearing his voice of tears.

"I went to visit my mom,
She was sick, did you get the letter?"

"I just got in, sweetheart I know,
things haven't been great
Haven't been what a true love marriage
Should be like, but it will be."

"I want this to work out,
I love you with all of me."
The weather of the night grew
Colder, but the heat of their love
Was shared in the darkness
Of the wintered house.

Storybook

A life exists, where stories,
Are the events and moments
Of her existence, stories of
Her birth to the burial of her
Body, she has the power to impact
The world with her life,
Which was made into a storybook,
Read to children or read by adults
She has found beauty and saved it,
A wintered rose growing in chaos,
A war for peace and safety
And the innocence of a child
Holding a weapon of destruction,
The river's reflection in the moon
And twinkling stars surrounding it
A life existed that turned to a tale,
A simple story that no one took it as
Truth, no one took as a true story,
The life of a woman
That gave inspiration to a storyteller,
A heart lies trapped in the grasp
Of a frozen lake, kept in a
Brush of color's love,
The storybook lies incomplete,
As the heart is kept out,
Feelings of the heart are frozen
By the winter's cold feathers,
The life went on with out the heart,
Without it being used,
In the story it doesn't say how she felt
That she yearned to be held by another,
Still it's a life we must note,

For the heart, even though frozen,
It floats around the still river,
But the storybook
Will always be incomplete, with every look
Into its story
Of the distant memory.

Chance Meeting

Have you ever heard of the sliding doors,
Where that one moment in life occurs,
And then again it doesn't,
A chance meeting with true love on the street
One door slides closing the miss,
It happened to me once, on a day
Where nothing was going right,
I woke up and saw my power was out
No light, no alarm clock to push me,
Got dressed in a hurry and ran to
The subway, just as I got there
I had found no money for faire,
I begged anyone to let me have a token
But it seemed that my words were broken,
Finally I just jumped over the rail
And ran to the train just as the
Sliding door had closed,
Arrived at work an hour and a half late,
This was fate,
For when I came home an hour and a half
Later, my eyes, my heart, they both saw
What I wished they wouldn't have,
My fiancé was in bed with another
Which was her lover,
Of several years, she kindly told me,
I had been thrown to the side
Just because I missed my ride,
It didn't make sense to me, why,
So she left, well actually, I left,
She kicked me out while tears
Where falling to the ground,
I went to a friend's house, hoping

He'd let me stay a bit,
As I was walking, I got hit
In the face by a swinging door
And fell right to the floor,
The woman felt bad about hitting me
As she ran over to me
Asking if I was alright, was I hurt, bleeding,
I told her I was fine, in that sense,
She told me her name was Lori,
And then it hit me, not the door, I knew
Her from college, and she recognized
My eyes, before I finish the first
Let me slide open the second,
It start out the same, wake up late,
Dressed in a hurry, subway, no faire,
But I get the train,
On the train I sit next to this woman,
She looked familiar, I just couldn't get it,
One of her books fell, I went to pick it up,
She jerked and kneed me in the face,
She asked if I was alright, hurt bleeding,
I told her I was fine,
She told me her name was Lori,
My college friend, I had so many classes
With her, right there, we talked
Until my stop, she gave me her number,
I came into work, everything was fine,
Left on my regular time,
Came home and saw my fiancé was
Still lying in bed, she said she was
Waiting for me, I have to skip a little,
Morning, Saturday sleep,
Anyway, I get up and see my fiancé
On the couch just lounging,

Relaxing in front of the TV, that's what I think
For a low voice, puts a little fear into the air,
I went back to my room, looking through
The want ads, trying to find another job,
She came in and said, she had to go out,
To the office, why do all of a sudden doubt
What ever she says,
I ask her, where she was really going,
She flips out and says I should be quite
Since I lost my job,
That I should be, lucky,
That she is not going to leave me,
She leaves in a hurry,
Or in furry,
I follow her to a bar,
And see, something I wish I hadn't,
I ran, thoughts going through my head,
How long,
Why,
I am so stupid not to have noticed earlier,
I thought she truly loved me,
No, she was playing with my heart
And never wanted to let go,
But I loved her so much,
Maybe I can just play it out,
Like I didn't see anything and
I will make things better,
I had to do it,
I ran to my friend's house
Snowy weather, slippery ice,
As I was crossing, the ice covered street,
A car slipped out of control, and hit me
Now I'm in the intensive care unit,
The first door, Lori and I still talked,

We talked about everything, even my ex-fiancé,
She told me to forget her, she was no good,
She put flaws into the flawless
Made the stars invincible
And the moon has a gloomy glow
Through the eyes, clear window
Is the key to love,
A kiss under the stars,
She apologized for the kiss
And ran to her high room,
As she left me standing, stunned,
Confused, not at all understanding what just happened,
The night was spent at my friend's
Morning, awake, I got dressed
And ran over to Lori's apartment,
For the kiss was in my mind,
I couldn't let go
I couldn't think of pain
Couldn't think of what my heart saw
Only of what my heart felt,
When she kissed me under those bright
Shinning stars, the kiss,
Snowy weather, slippery ice,
As I was crossing the ice covered street
A car slipped out of control and hit me,
The thing about the sliding doors,
In the end, one will close, the other to stay
Open to the stars and flawless moon,
It's better to know,
For that destined chance meeting
Will come around soon,
The second door closes on the flaws
For who needs, those imperfections,
A chance meeting happens to get rid

That drinking glass, that distorts
The true image, of the stars and the moon,
Love to be the savior of a heart,
An end to one door,
But to continue, with the other,
Sliding doors of life.

Death Of Inspiration

No more can I look into its eyes
And picture a sweet dream in words,
I stare blankly at my surroundings
And feel emptiness,
I feel my heart wanting to confess
To my mind, the disease that is taking,
Breaking
Into the center of creation,
I feel all around me, the death of inspiration,
No more can I see the bloom of winter
Or the feeling of love within a splinter,
Speck, grain of any heart
Whether it is big or small
Warm or cold,
I would be able to hear
The single drop of a tear,
I can't experience that anymore,
Within the blur of time
I am trapped, empty of words,
The power to move a crowd
Of stiff hearts, lost
The power to create emotion
When all is lost,
That to is lost,
My hand clutches the pen
Squeezing it, hoping that a drop of ink
Would inspire, but all it does, is sink
Into the paper, now with a drop
Of nothing taking up the space
Of creation
Without any kind of inspiration
I feel the burden of a life

That holds no beauty
In the ugliness of life,
Inspiration to write, to see, to live,
And once again, to love.

Shadow Of A Rose

A darkened reflection of beauty
Poses its figure on the concrete,
Its shadow, is cast by the bright glow
Of the moon that rests incomplete,
In the shadow grows
Emotions of every, and any kind,
Hidden is a scar that all laughed, and whispered at
For it is time in rewind,
The rose hides in her shadow
Fearing to come out into the light,
Life lived in shadow throwing out
Sun fires, and pictures of the majestic moonlight,
She doesn't talk or show herself to anyone
For the shadow keeps her hidden,
She thinks she lives happily ever after
Now that she is within
The shadow of her own being
Which is the rose,
In the light, stand still, no one can
See the beauty, watch her in pose
Left everyone breathless, strike a pose,
Left all eyes empty of her fragrant touch
That stills his heart,
Ran away into her shadow's keep
For she is lost when the moon's counterpart
Appears in the lighter of days,
Still I feel she is in shadow
Every minute of her life
She never does plan to show
Her eyes to the likes of her
Or even to him,
Doesn't matter if she finds happiness in light

Or even if the candle grows dim,
She is the most beautiful creature
Of a chaotic step in rain
Still she lives under the shadow
Living in a chaotic step of pain.

Little Alexes

Little Alexes grew up watching her
Much older sister
Growing up in a faster lane,
Speeding through the stop signs
And crossing solid lines,
Little Alexes was very timid, hard to break
And with the rules of her parents
And off-course the world
She would comply,
A cute girl with aspirations of being different,
She saw the world differently,
From her point of view
Beauty could be seen on cue,
With the shatter of eye lids,
Beauty would rise,
Sitting in her room, Alexes would listen
To the conversations her sister
Would be having,
Writing down her emotions
And what she was thinking at that
Second, Moment, Hour, Month, Year,
Her whole life was starting to
Fill up books upon books,
Sometimes her emotions would be hidden,
Still there in the context
Of her little stories,
She produced words of passion
As well as compassion,
Little Alexes wrote her heart out
Threw it on paper,
Her love of things
Her hate of the cold weather

But the silky feel of a feather,
The feather brushing against her
Slowly, a fantasy she wants,
Her dreams and reality moments
Are all in her books,
Closed to the world,
But open to little Alexes
To read over and over,
In one of her stories
Alexes wanted her sister's life,
Where the guy she dreamed of
Would find her irresistible
And unforgettable under the
Night's passionate starry sky,
Little Alexes desired the touch
Of his lips and his hand on her,
Her emotions became complex,
Started looking on to the safer sex,
Her emotions became her one emotion,
A mind and heart living in commotion
Of a story that never ended in her book,
Unfortunately it was never a story
To tell as if it had a rose to bloom,
Hidden away in her memory
Is the end,
Shadow cast in open ground
She faced her horror alone,
A ghostly story that haunts
The crackling campfire
Little Alexes reaches the chaotic age,
18 fills a 20 page
Novel of feelings of her own
Experiences and demons,
She also lives in the steps of her

Other sister, now 22,
A very beautiful girl, still
With those aspirations of being different,
She becomes a usual person to hang
Around a bar listening to the live bands,
Under the shadowed moon
She cries out for one,
A guy in the band, the lead singer,
She waves her arms around
Showing off her addiction,
Her feelings in the written word
Becomes twisted and blurred
By irreversible takes of demons
Idiocracy becomes her habit,
Lead singer finds Little Alexes
At the back of the bar,
Cold to the warmest of touches,
The moon frowns to the sight
Seen in the back of the bar,
Books of twisted emotions and
Strait emotions published,
Different in so many ways,
But then again,
She fell to the same idiocracy.

Bucket Beats

Walk along Time Square,
Take out your train faire
As you walk down to the platform,
Listen to the beats coming in thunderous storm,
Listen to the beats echo off the walls
And towering buildings, hear the beat calls,
Hands or broken broom sticks
Beat the buckets to a certain rhythm of tricks,
Stop and give your ears a listen,
So what if the player doesn't glisten,
Listen to the rhythm-tick
And watch not one stick,
But both at the same time,
Don't drop one dime
But a hundred of them,
Giving thanks to the rhythm
Beat out by street players on bucket beats,
Listen to the rhythm of the streets,
30 blocks away
You know the bucket beats are at play,
Faster and faster the sticks become thin air
Faster and faster, it was like they were never there
Beat after beat I have it in my ears
Played out through their hearts and tears,
No signature on the dotted line
They play their heart out under the six train sign,
The rhythm from those bucket beats
Puts motion in the streets
Keeping them alive with the culture verses
Instead of those slang filled verses,
Is that even a word,
For shizzel, is that what I just heard,

Bucket beats save our ears
And our hearts filled with musical fears
Of where hip hop is going,
It doesn't seem like we're growing,
We're flowing
Down instead of up in age
And more with rage,
Bucket beats,
Save our dying streets.

Game In The Park

Do you feel free now that your feelings were said,
Expressed in the open park, hurt bled
Through the eyes of the broken,
You think heads or tails as you flip the token,
Whether you choose one or the other
You turn up alone, without one, or the other,
You always take them to the park in front of a crowd
Thinking she won't scream or cry as loud,
Why do you do it to her, her, her, and her,
Do they all become a blur
The moment, no the second you say goodbye,
Or is it when you sea the tear of a cry
That all those memories along with that heart,
Will completely disappear, depart
On the nine o'clock train, to where
Do you dare
To ask what will become of her
No, you stick with that blur,
Never thinking about that heart anymore
Gone previous to the tear hitting the floor,
It's a game played n the park
In the light or in the dark
Where a heart is told a story of the falling moon,
Whether it falls to the sea or land, it shall fall soon,
The blurs, the feelings, the expressions
Will all be just an impression,
One day you wake up, you truly open your eyes
And remember all the cries,
Those of your own, those of love,
Pushed away with a shove
Discover the reason
After the end of the season,
Bleeding heart bleeds out for her,
That last blur.

A Story Of Love And Hatred

Clouds turn black for mourn
As tears are about to be born,
Those tears soak into our bleeding hearts,
Clothes of the darkened clouds
Worn surrounding a casket
That is slowly being lowered to the sky,
Family and friends stand soaking
In the rain of tears,
Whispers of questions speed around
As to whom that girl is
Standing in a puddle of her own cries,
Unfamiliar eyes
Are hidden behind dark tinted glasses,
The grandson of the man who passed
Overheard the whispers surrounding the service,
With his own pair of curious and
Wondering eyes, he approaches,
The whispering stops
As the service ends,
The grandson introduced himself
As Wintered Heart, grandson
Of the late Poetic Heart, saying it sadly
And with pride, to be his grandson,
She introduced herself as Ria Sims
An old friend of Poetic,
Wintered asked Ria how they met,
She replied saying it was too long of a story,
Wintered urged her to go ahead,
They walked along the saddened passes
As she started her story,
I knew Poetic from a friend
Didn't really think much of him,

He was funny and full of energy,
At the time I was in a frightening
Relationship, with a man that beat fear
Into my body,
I was supposed to be engaged to him
For deep inside, I did love him,
It was just that he changed
Since the first time we kissed,
I wanted to get out
And be with someone else,
I felt like I was trapped
The moon trapped in the web of stars,
Once and a while, I would escape
Into the fast pace life
Leaving for a day or two,
But I'd have to come back,
I saw Poetic after he moved away,
He came along to say hello
And I noticed him,
The romantic passion in a light so dim,
He was so stunning,
Can you say that about a guy,
He was so strong and handsome,
I sensed romance, passion, and pain,
I asked my friend about his heart
Wanting to know more
Wanting to know how he worked
How his heart beats,
She gave me his phone number,
I couldn't wait to call,
He didn't pick up,
Crushed hopes, fantasies,
I tried again, after I came home
From escaping fear a bit,

We talked for three hours
About everything and anything,
The next night we talked for two,
He asked if anything can become of us,
I told him no, I had Fear
And I was scared to leave him,
Thoughts of what could be
What the moon could see,
We decided to meet in the fast pace
Around two, when the sun was out,
We fell into each others eyes
Loosing the sense of fear
And the sense that it could never be,
Passionate kisses and hugs
I felt safe within his keep,
I didn't expect to fall for him,
Never did I ever imagine it
To come true,
I was lost in his eyes so blue,
We went home around two
When the moon show it's brightest,
I wanted to see him the next day
To be in his arms,
Once again, so I wouldn't loose the feeling
Or the sweet smell of him on my clothes,
And to be lost in his big blue bright eyes,
He called the next day
And I told my father to lie
To say I wasn't there,
He called the day after
And I picked up, I was scared
To tell him I didn't want to be
With his eyes and heart,
But then again I did,

I told him he was a player,
It was a lie,
I told him I still loved Fear,
It was a lie,
I told him my father would
Kick me out, throw me on the street
If I had not forgotten about Poetic,
And to marry into Fear,
That, was the truth,
I had hurt him
And I didn't mean to,
The next day
I called him
But he didn't pick up,
I told him I would call again,
He picked up the second time
And I told him I needed
The CD I lent him,
I really just wanted to see him again
To look into those eyes of his
Once more, just to be lost,
I told him I didn't expect this,
Never did I imagine my fantasy
To be true to life,
We said our goodbyes
Under the train station
That went to the fast pace,
I would ask my friend
If she saw Poetic,
He never did leave my mind
Or my heart,
It was love, at first date,
A fantasy, that could never be,
Wintered asked what happened with her

And her forced love Fear,
She replied
He is no longer in my life,
For fear grew too much for me to stay alive,
Wintered gave her a sealed note
With Poetic's signature on it
Addressed to a woman with red hair
And covered eyes,
Ria read the note
And said thank you to Wintered
And started to walk away,
Wintered ran after her
Asking what the letter said,
What his grandfather wrote,
She said he wrote, he hated
What I did, and the fantasy
Did come true,
Fantasies are a one day thing,
She hugged Wintered
And took off her tinted covers,
With a smile in her eyes
She said,
You have his eyes,
She covered her eyes
Turned,
And walked away,
Clutching the note,
Off-course she is known
To lie twice, before,
Telling the truth.

Reading

Midnight sky reflected
On the ocean water,
Blistering stars surround
Their king the moon
Seen by a pair of eyes, from the sand,
Questions and concerns, fill his mind
And fill his already heavy heart,
He walks along the ocean crashes
Where he is under the mysterious spell
Of the full moon, so big
It seems so close,
He steps on the face cover
Of a worn out book,
"Poetic Tales From Poetic Heart"
He decided to take a look
Into what was contained
In his finding,
He turned to the first page
And read;

Under the pale moon I see her eyes,
Under the pale moon I see her beauty,
Under the pale moon she has no disguise,
For under the pale moon, I express myself truly.

He read on finding more intense words
More power and passion,
He kept going and going
Not being able to stop,
Intensity and passion, he admired
What he read, admired the expression,
Love made sense, the moon

And the blistering stars reflected
Onto the ocean water,
Made complete sense,
For finally he saw answers
To questions of his worries,
He came up closer to the water
And let the ocean touch his feet,
The cold, yet warm feel of the deepened blue
Put a smile in his eyes,
He continued to read this poetry
That has stunned him
Beneath the moon, his eyes,
Got brighter and bigger,
With the help of the midnight sky,
His heart was beating differently,
For those words
That he couldn't stop reading
Until the rise of the sun,
Had answered what he had pondered,
They were answers in the sand,
He understood why it was so worn out,
Giving his thoughts no doubt
He laid the book down
On the sandy beach,
Covered it slightly, and left,
Giving someone else a chance
And pleasure of reading,
Poems of love, fear, hatred, and sadness,
Doesn't matter what he questioned,
He found his answers
In the words of Poetic Heart,
Passion, beauty, night, day, stars, and
The slightly covered moon.

Tears In Blood

The sound of a slamming door
Echoes through the hallways,
Over and over again,
The moonlight shines in through the window
Onto a bath of tears,
Slowly soaking into the bed
Staining strait through the protective sheets,
Tears drop in the way of a dark winter snowfall,
Featherlike, but stained red,
Speculation of what occurred, varied in words,
Whether it was under the spell of the moon
Or in the fiery passion of the sun,
The bath of tears lingered round
Never completely soaking into the bed,
The one body was stained with agonizing pain
For tears poured out like river drain,
But still, they're stained in red,
Tears come seeping out of the eye
That leads to the heart,
And that, goes back up to the mind,
What is there, hidden in the dormant light
Until the clap of thunder,
And it's awake,
What is it, when someone has no more tears,
Does it mean no fears,
Absolutely no worries,
A mind, stays empty of snow flurries,
Or is that they have all been drained out,
All that is left, is the flow
Of a body's river,
Pumping throughout the eyes,
Heart, and its mind,

All that is left, is blood,
Or maybe another conclusion,
The tears in blood
Slowly, or in a quick pace
Pour out onto the bed,
The eyes still have tears to shed,
But cries, out tears in blood instead
Staining her comfort,
Whether under the spell of the moon
Or in the fiery passion of the sun,
Those tears stain, soak, and stay.

Standing In The Rain

First day of April
And arrive the April showers
Leaking down the tall towers,
Each drop hits my bare
Face and hands,
Have enough sense to
Stand in the rain,
For without a single care in
The chaotic and distraught world,
I stand in the rain,
Feeling the light
Or the heavy tears of the sky,
Listening to the silent thunder
And flashing lightning
That lights up the entire night sky,
Moonlit, yet, still it rains,
My heart feels no drop,
For I don't beg it to stop,
Why run away,
Why hide under the concrete covers,
They will leak in the rain
And then what,
Feel the rain drip into you,
Feel the splash of a puddle,
Be light on your feet
And sing like Fred Estair
I know why he sang,
Happiness grew over him,
Not at all dim,
Bright, shinning through
Even though rain poured,
What a glorious feeling

To know someone is interested
In getting to know
Your likes, dislikes,
Everything that makes you,
You, and nothing less,
You get the feeling to confess
That it is she that is
Always on your mind,
Can't stop though of her smile,
The sound of her voice
Still echoes in your ears
And that is the pouring rain,
With every sound,
All you hear is her angelic voice,
Soothing your heart
And lightening up your eyes,
Stand in the rain,
And I'll know why you do so,
Drenched, in wet happiness,
Dance, stump your feet in the puddle,
Be free to sing
Your heart out to her,
Let it be known
That the stars found each other
In the covered sky,
For even though blind,
They find
Each other on a friendship course
That turns into more,
Maybe a sliding door
That finally opened,
The rain beats off me
And I just stand there,
Still with those thoughts,

That voice,
I found happiness again,
I found a way to smile,
For now I have no sense
To come out of the rain,
For if I do,
I am senseless.

What For, I Ask

How often do think about it,
How often do you stay in that pit,
Ideas and thoughts racing in your mind
The answers, you can never find,
Do you stare at the reflection in the stained steel
Do you conceal,
Yourself within the deep thought,
Have you fought
Intensely to escape the drugged belief,
Is it brief,
Why do your lips struggle to smile,
Lay on the floor fogging up the bathroom tile,
What part do you want to end,
Exactly what do you intend
To permanently stop,
POP,
Oh, you scared me, I thought you were done with,
You know, then you'd become that myth
That fades after awhile,
Why don't you smile,
Are you trying to keep in image of yourself,
Your smile, is a dusty book resting on its shelf,
What for, I have to ask,
Do you want to, perform this task
That you have marinating in your trembling hand
And there it is, a question buried in the sand,
Is there anything worth saying alive for,
Do you confuse the metaphor, of the swinging door
To death,
To taking your final breath
Before you exit, stage right,
Wouldn't you miss the moonlight

And the wintered trees,
Falling leaves and springing back, your memories
All would be lost,
That is the cost
To putting an end to this, and more ahead,
Yu might be able to live outside the tear shed,
What about her,
Do you want that to become a blur
In those eyes, and heart,
A new life she would have to start
Without you in her thought,
Escape, don't stay caught
In the reflection,
Don't consider death as life's perfection,
What for, I ask,
Nothing to say, now remove your mask.

A Series Of Heightened Senses

H.D. Balzac once said, "Love is poetry of the senses"
An interesting quote, but
What if one was dead from senses
If one couldn't smell a flower,
Couldn't feel the touch of her lips,
Or couldn't taste sweetness on their tongue,
How would they know love?
Let's take a glimpse outside the diner.

I

Outside The Diner

The steam, from the hot cup of coffee
Rises, into the blurred vision of a man
Sitting in a booth,
In the back of a Manhattan diner,
An angelic voice comes from behind,
"Would that be all Poetic?"
The man nods his head yes
And says "Just a check please."
He sits, back toward the entrance
Toward everyone in the diner,
"Here's the check Poetic, thank you."
"Excuse me, can I…
Oh never mind, thank you."
The waitress leaves with a pondering look,
He sits tapping his foot, on the floor of the busy
Yet slow diner,
He leaves the money and walks for the door,
As he's about to leave, the waitress stops his exit,
"Poetic, what did you want to ask me?"
"Nothing, I was just wondering about something."

"About what?"
"Please, I have to go."
"She steps aside and says, "Come back soon."
He stares into her eyes
A second that felt like an eternity
Lost, he wakes from her blink,
Then walks out,
He takes the three stairs that led down
To the sidewalk, slowly,
Shifting eyes from left to right,
Shifting hours, from day to night,
His feet take him back to work
Then back home,
For his question never left the booth,
He sits in his armchair, in his apartment
Doubting himself
Sinking into his chair deeper and deeper,
Sinking into love, deeper and deeper,
Eight am, morning wake
He rises to the sound of courage, confidence,
Confident on the way out the door,
Confident on the walk,
Confident on the train,
Where is confidence to be found now,
As he stands shaking
Outside the diner,
Sweating palms, nervous heart,
Outside the diner,
From inside his head,
A voice comes, breaking through the winter ice.

"Why are you just standing there?
Move,
Go in, open the door,

Let your words run free,
Let your lips flap wildly into the breeze,
Get in the diner,
Find her eyes in yours
And confess,
Love is poetry of the senses
Love sets you free
Love gives you wings,
Geronimo,
Step one,
Step two,
Step three,
Get in the diner
Your alarm is screaming at max volume,
Don't hit the snooze
Get up and look deep into her heart
Through her blue windows,
Throw your worries out,
Barge in, don't knock first,
Take her to the side
And tell her she is why you come in,
She is why you drink that cup
Of steaming hot coffee,
The pain of burning your tongue
Is worth just to see her,
Stop shaking and go in
Hide your fear,
Take a chance
For they rarely come along."

So there he stands,
In the past he folded all his hands,
Stands, outside the diner,
Ten minute, no move,

Not even a blink,
For he stares at the swinging door,
Nervousness freezes his body
It puts a cold stillness upon him,
"Hey Poetic, how are you?"
He wakes up from his nervous state
And sees an old friend,
"River, I've been good, you?"
"I've been great, getting married,
Next month,
Met her at the train station,
Its, like, I just had the chance,
And I didn't freeze,
After I asked her out
Everything started to fall
Into place,
Outside the train, that I almost missed,
I decided that being scared
Isn't worth missing out on finding
Love,
Have you ever heard
That love, is poetry of the senses,
Without those senses,
I felt transparent
Non existent,
We were both the same,
Fear puts you into death,
Poetry makes you feel alive,
Hey Poetic, here's my card,
Call me, I would really like
To keep in touch."
"Okay, I'll call you."
They shook hands,
River went on his way,

Poetic took all what River said,
Step one,
Step two,
Step three,
He opens the door, free
Of fear, well, sort of,
He finds his waitress
And confesses
"I love you,
You are poetry in all ways,
You put my senses in motion,
I come in here just to see,
Just to hear your voice,
The scent of your perfume
Pumps my heart,
Love, is poetry of the senses,
And I can't help
Wanting my senses,
To be set free,
I love you,
I found this out two years ago,
Outside that diner
I stood
Scared, I should
Have asked a long time,
Ago, you are my sense's rhyme,
I love you."
The waitress smiled
As the whole diner's
Busy, yet silent
Eyes stared, as the two
Shared romantic moments
In each others closed eyes
In each others lips,

Love is definitely poetry of the senses,
Inside, the diner.
What strikes a sense to awaken
From deep slumber, scent
Touch of true love passing by,
One's eyes have to pay attention,
For if your heart comes to life
From the sense of poetry, act upon it,
A glimpse outside the train.

II

River's Romance

River runs dry, of emotion,
For he is the shallow ocean,
Even at the striking sight of the moon
He thinks, of how soon
His eyes, should close
And be in the mid-night pose,
No sight or smell strikes a sense
For he awakes tense,
Blank look as he walks to the train
With no feeling of joy or pain.

There he stands
Blank stare, at a blank wall,
"oh I'm sorry sir"
No response, to an apology for a push,
A rarity on the platform
Where rushing feet and java steam
Fills the train station,
Busy eyes, feet, hands, and bodies
Except for River,
Morning paper or the morning breakfast bar

To the day long, blank,
He walks up and down his schedule
Going along with those ordinary thoughts
And so called dreams.

Train arrives as he boards the back cart
The back booth,
Looking past his reflection
In the pitch black window,
"Good morning River."
"Hey River, what's up?"
"Yo nice suit River."
Never said, as he walks into work,
A mere head nod
From his friend and co-worker Poetic,
Almost on the same emotional level,
Fear is the only thing that lives
Inside both their beat less hearts,
Winter of the four seasons
Freezes, takes the warmth out,
They wouldn't put up a fight, or even shout
In the emotion of anger.

So there he stands, awaiting the train,
Living a life considered as plain
And uneventful,
He takes a deep breath
Simultaneously a floating Petal walks by,
Striking a sense
That makes his heart beat,
Not slow, but a fast pace,
Quickly turns his head to see the scent
Of Petal Rose,
His eyes could not close

Not even blink
A second of time,
For every move, was her rhyme
To her own self,
The smell of her
Made his heart go bump, bump,
The sight of her
Made his heart go bump, bump,
The sound of her saying "excuse me."
Made his heart go bump, bump,
He wanted to know about
The touch and the taste of her,
For sure, it would make his senses
Go wild,
He took his first step toward her
As the train arrived, but it was a blur
She made no advance toward the train
As he continued to approach,
He tapped her on the shoulder
To gain, her attention,
His opening line caught her, fully.

"Excuse me, I just wanted to say,
You brought me to life,
For it was your scent, sight, and sound
That made my heart
Finally beat,
For the first time
I felt, my senses
I felt emotion, that I have never felt,
You made the ice on my heart melt,
It was you that put my senses
Into flow of,
A River that finally moves,

A heart, mind, face never again to be in a single pose,
I couldn't let you go without saying this
For you brought me into life,
Into poetry of the senses,
Can I hear your name."

"Petal Rose."

"Uh, my heart beats faster."
As she giggles.

"Please don't continue,
You're embarrassing me."

"Can I have your number,
So we can meet again
Under the moon,
The striking mid-night moon."
She said yes
As River puts his hand over
His own beating heart,
She handed her number to him,
I'll call you soon,
Is that all right?"

"Yes, I would like that."

"Wow, thank you,
I have to catch my train now,
That is closing its doors
I'll call you later Petal."
He ran and barely made it on,
He stood in a different cart,
Smile on his face

He came into work
And walked straight into his boss's office,
"No longer can I work here
I quit."
He left to clean out his desk
And came up to Poetic
Who was starring outside the window
At the footsteps of a diner,
"Poetic, I just quit this job,
You should leave as well.
This place makes you mindless, unconscious,
Did you hear me at all?
What are you staring at?"

"Nothing, I, I'm just looking."

"Well I have to get out, hope you snap out of it soon."
River shook Poetic's hand
And said goodbye,
He left smiling,
Saying to himself
Rose and Love are both poetry
For they both heighten the senses.

What if one thought their senses alive,
Felt emotion of a dark hand
Always, following her steps,
Would that one heart realize true poetry
When walked in, breaking through darkness,
Another glimpse, into the diner.

III
Floetic Problems

Her eyes slowly open
From an un-restful slumber,
She turns her fluttering eyes toward
Her red, glowing alarm clock
Screaming you're late,
She springs out from bed
Only if she cared,
Five minutes later, she's finally awake
Ready to take a shower,
A half hour later she's putting on her shoes
At the door, a frame with a picture
Hung for remembrance, and mourn,
The middle part taken out, torn
Out, to forget,
She steps out into a sudden downpour,
Her heart aches, soar
From the pain of loss,
she gets to work an hour late
And comfort given from
Her boss, co-worker, and customer.

"Can I help you sir?"

"Yes, French toast please and a cup of coffee."

"French toast for the back table."
She tried so hard not to crack,
Burst tears into a bowl
Made from her hands put together,
She hung depression
Right on her face as she brought the coffee.

"Are you alright?"

"To tell you the truth, I'm not alright
I where clothes of the night
I where my struggling fight
On my face when I'm asleep
And when I'm awake,
Sorry, do you really want to know this?"
The man just nods his head,
"Well I have problems, disturbing
My once happy floe."

"Why don't you sit down."
She smiled

"Thanks, but I have to get back to work."

"Okay, no problem,
My name is Poetic Heart."

Mine's Floetic Love,
Thanks for listening."
An hour after Poetic left
Frozen Flow, her supposed love
Of three years, came in to the diner,
And all he has is promises and forced tears,
Threats on Floetic's heart
Said in a loud thunderous clap,
She shook every time
Frozen came into her sight,
Every time he spent the night,
No comfort, no ease
Given by the supposed love
Of Frozen, of his iced heart,

A chill breath, when he speaks,

"Why didn't you pick up last night,
What was so important,
Why do I even bother with you,
Your parents died, so what,
You better pick up tonight
Or else, your heart will find light dim,
Your eyes shall not blink
Or open, from a night's sleep, ever again."

NO, its over Frozen."
All he could do was stare with his flaring eyes,
Curved lips, and tight fists,
"its over Frozen,
I'm running away from your
Thunderous threats and unloving arms,
No more, never again,
Now leave
If you don't there will be trouble."
Frozen turned and stormed out the door
As a co-worker offered her apartment
To stay in for as long as she needs,
Sometimes being alone is not a good thing.

The same customer came in
On the next day, to the next,
Ordering French toast, and coffee
In the busy,
Yet slow NYC diner,
She didn't show a smile
Till there he was
Day after day,
Breakfast and lunch,
Words, smiles, laughs
Her floetic problems

Of a loss, and fears of hurt
That changed her life
From easy to strife,
Is slowly going away
Day after day,
Just from talking
In the back booth
At the back of the diner,
She came up to her co-worker and confessed

"I'm in love,
With that guy that comes in everyday,
Ordering the same thing
Is sit waiting
Turning my head every time
I hear the door open,
Either someone coming in
Or leaving,
I turn to sea if its him,
Even if he left,
Hoping he'll come into confess
Maybe he is in love as well,
I wait for the jingle of the door's bell
To see Poetic,
Even though the same time
Every day, like a poem's obvious rhyme,
I wait and on my days off
I miss him,
I love him,
Two years ago he made me smile
When no one else could,
And it hasn't stopped ever since."

The co-worker smiled and said,

"Go for it honey,
Confess what you confessed to me
Right to him,
Deliver it to his heart."

"you think he loves me too."

How will you know unless,
You tell him, if you love him
Let him know, he comes in here never missing a day,
Probably just to come and see you."
The next day Poetic came in and said hello to Floetic
And went to his booth,
They talked and talked
She couldn't ask,
Fear of him saying no,
Put her in a scared flow,

"Would that be all Poetic?"
He nods his head yes
And says "Just a check please."
She went to get the check
And was shaking, still scared,
She looked at her co-worker
As she signaled her to confess,
Floetic nodded her head,

"Here's the check Poetic, thank you."
"Excuse me, can I…
Oh never mind, thank you."
Floetic leaves with a pondering look,

"Why didn't you tell him Floetic,
Come on, don't miss out on this chance

For a real love, unthreatened."
Floetic stood silent,
As he was about to leave, Floetic stopped his exit
"Poetic, what did you want to ask me?"
"Nothing, I was just wondering about something."
"About what?"
"Please, I have to go."
"She steps aside and says, "Come back soon."
She stares into his eyes
And he walks out
As her heart drops down and squeezes inside her little toe.

The next day she is more nervous than ever,
Noticing, at that obvious rhyme
The door did not open
Poetic did not come in,
And walk to the back of the diner
To sit, in the back booth,
The door opened
As she didn't look,
Given up on that he might come in
But, it was Poetic, he grabbed her and confessed
His love, his passionate love to her,
They both smiled
As the whole diner
Busy, yet silent,
Stared as the two
Shared romantics moments,
The Poetic Floetic of a heart feels Love,
As the river carries the Petal of a Rose,

Love is poetry of the senses,
You just have to find it
Amongst the frozen.

Not My Fight

Explosions, is my alarm clock,
For in each block
Of time, I'm trapped in war,
Deepest, darkest thoughts to explore,
This is not y fight,
Still I have to kill under the moonlight
Which should be admired, never ignored,
The sounds of gun shots poured
Into my already pounding head,
For the wet marshes are my bed,
Rain comes down from the eyes of those
We killed and are now laying in a restful pose,
Stay hidden, stay low,
For no enemy eye to see, do not show
Your obvious fear,
Not my fight m let me disappear,
Let me go back home, to love, my wife,
Let me live my life,
Why do I have to kill Vietnam, why
They are killing us, the Americans cry,
Explosions, where am I, water cage,
I hear footsteps on the wooden plank, turn the page,
I shake in fear of what is next to come,
They feed us by the crumb,
To barely keep us breathing, alive,
No way to survive,
This is not my fight, still
I do kill,
Now I'm caught in the enemy's hand,
Pain comes out, throwing burning hot sand
Into my eyes,
Cries

Yelling for help, to be saved,
Or will I sink into the watery grave,
Not my fight,
Or is it, who is wrong, who is right,
Is it the free loving rebels, living life pearled,
Or the tight politicians of the so called, free world,
Who cares, my life is done,
Killed, a war we could have never won.

Life Is Pleasure

Life is pleasure,
But still, tears are falling
Fear is stalking
Our hearts,
Our minds,
And our souls
Looking around, every corner
Making sure its safe,
Before we step,
I still want to live
Still, want to see the sun up
To the sundown,
Life is pleasure,
So why don't we feel it
Only feel strife,
But go along with it,
Down, the river of life
For I can't see the sun
Ruled by the cloudy and rainy days,
Let me, go through
That open door
Onto, the other side
Of the bright shining stars,
That's our distant universal dream
Where they, do have that chance
To come into focus of reality,
Behind all the dark clouds
And all, those thunderous storms,
Lies the bright orange sunset
Kisses, under the bright glow
Of the moon,
That is nested, in the stars

Our dreams, untouched
By hands, of a stranger's kind,
We go on, hoping that star
To come down close enough,
To, reach our hand
To that moonlit, starlit
Midnight glow sky,
Of a world where dreams
Can and do come true,
We don't have to live
A life, of a Disney cartoon
To achieve that desire,
To see our dreams
In realities, bright eyes,
Life is pleasure,
If one can find
Something, in those clouds
In the raindrops,
Tears of the sky
Can be, tears of happiness
For every time it rains,
A dream will, find its way,
Down into the eyes,
Of reality.

Library Hall

I read through these, classic words,
The aged words, of great minds,
The romantic words, of Shakespeare
Imagery portrayed
By the words, of William Blake
Millions of books, of the old way
And of today,
I read and wonder
Can, my poetry be compared
Even, thought of
When talking in tricks of literature,
Even in, the present poetic rhyme,
Maya Angelou and Robert Frost in my time,
Am I just as good,
Can I write, the beauty of a kiss
To the point where, readers are stunned,
By the words, put together
That no one could have thought of,
Then again, I can
I am not like the great poets,
Of the far and near past,
I am of the present,
Shakespeare, Keats, Browning, Angelou, Frost
I am different,
My style can still stun a kiss,
For I can, put simple words
Together, to stun and inspire,
For one day another, will come along
And ask, if they,
Can write like me.

Stage Lighted Smile

Broken words leads, to broken hearts
Look under the clouds,
At this darkened world,
All around, are stage lighted smiles
Hiding in dark corners,
Are their true problems
That want, to be undercover
Wanting people to, leave them alone,
Not wanting those, concerned questions,
Are you okay,
Do you want to talk,
Hey, let's take a walk,
You can discuss with me
All that, is bothering you,
All these things, that stress
And put life, in a mess,
No, I really am fine
You try to nicely decline,
But they still persist,
With come on, I'll buy you a cup of coffee
Here's my number, call me,
Once again, you nicely decline
But, they still come with
Let's go out tonight,
Have some fun, and forget,
But, the stage is set
For there is a smile to hide,
What is truly on their mind
What is, stuck, what break their heart,
The show, A Stage Lighted Smile
So often, you would think, it's in style,
Seeing them, on all different faces,

In those darkened corners
Are, the hidden frowns,
What would happen if
Everyday life was filled with stress
On every single heart,
Of the living
Keeping, everyone away,
From a true smile
Can things, get that bad
To keep everyone sad,
Having those faint smiles
Closing down, on the bright moon
Giving, nothing away,
Do you have a stage lighted smile
That can fool any eye,
Behind closed doors
Lies, the true feelings
That can't be seen, outside,
That lie bare, it doesn't hide
It cries, echoes through the hall,
So make a call,
Go out for coffee
Talk
Take a simple walk,
Ringing bells of a door,
Or red, painted on the floor,
Tears fall like a rainy storm,
From eyes that understand pain,
Eyes that can't see
The beauty of the night
The moonlight,
It's so far out of sight,
For held thoughts and words
Never expressed,

Pressed down, hard, on a feeble heart,
A stage lighted smile
Gets its, standing ovation
As, the lights dim,
Curtains close,
Seats are empty,
Here comes the beauty of the night.

A Sad Girl I Know

Inspired by Laura Gofryk

The bare Manhattan streets, hold heavy steps
Of a heavy hearted girl
With eyes, of a rumbling storm,
On par with the falling leaves, raindrops
Pour from her eyes onto past cemented tears,
She walks, clouds to the streets,
Even in a sea of people, she feels alone,
A black rose trembles in the gusting wind,
She walks by Roxy's glancing at her sadness
In the reflective windows,
She's almost at Central Park, her saddened tear,
Continue to fall onto the streets
Running a river of breadcrumbs back to pain,
She enters by the pond
And walks into a shower of Fall's leaves,
And she seas, her past memories,
In between the brown, dead, dry, tear leaves,
She falls to her knees, as her tears burst
Into artic ice over the pond,
Winter's first snowfall comes
As she waits, for winter to pass,
Leaving her in sunlight, in the park's arms,
This sad girl I know, wants so much
For new memories to be made,
An image in the falling leaves, speaks
"Don't be afraid, my daughter
No sadness upon my departure,
I lived the best, I could,
Smile, in my absence
Only remember, do not mourn

Do not stay in the shadows,
Come into the light, and live
My beautiful, sun-filled girl."
A final tear, drops from her cheek
Onto her open palm, closed tight
And kept, in her memories,
No longer heavy hearted, a true smile
For all, to love and see.

Empty Quotes

Now, where do I go from here,
For I can't find, the bright verse in the night,
I don't want to force her sad tear,
My heart and mind struggle, they stay in the grueling fight
Since she believes, that I am the one,
No other does she want to love, she wants me
But, it's my heart, that is telling me to run,
It is the harsh reality
That my mind, keeps going over with my heart,
Do I love her, I can't seem to find it again
Can't find that spark, or the start
Of that loving feeling, lost in silence, and then
Quotes to love, now lie empty
In my mouth, she has to live a life, without me.

Again Silent

My loud voice has grown silent,
For at this moment
My eyes, speak louder
Than I could ever scream,
A figure in the doorway
With hair flowing, to her troubled shoulders,
And lips, I'm nervous to taste,
In that moment, my eyes are
Again silent.

A Walk Pass Dark Doors

"Why do they hate me?"
A tall, abnormally shaped and feared figure
Walks, pass securely locked doors and shutters,
Dragging his feet along the pebbled road
Murmuring, grunting, sifting through the night,
Like a deep drunk in still thought,
He continues to pass by darker doors.

"Why fear me, when I walk near
Why run when I show face
In the dimmest of moonlights,
Am I, the opposite of that velvet rose,
Today's occurrence, was the worst I felt,
Never have I saw such fear
In the eyes of innocent and guilty,
The sun moved away, to hide, from what it feared
And fled, ran screaming, looking for safety
In the arms of their mothers or love,
What did I do, I heard a storm
Of thundering footsteps, but no lightning,
Might it have been the stained red
On my torn, dirty clothing,
Did they fear that, or was it my whole image,
My hideous look, my painful face,
Hidden in shadow, they run in fear,
The footsteps ceased, as I heard echoes,
Echoing through the thick alley of doors
Were those locks, turning and dropping,
They run from fear, I know why,
The red stain, is not my own,
I am the reason, for her last scream."
Footsteps shuffle, pass each dark door.

Brightest Stars

Follow the brightest stars to get
Back to my heart,
A path, leading not to darkness
In the cold,
A path only to get brighter, from your
Wide open eyes,
Follow the path with no fear that will
Close, your blue windows,
Believe me, when I say, the path
Will
And the path can, get only brighter
As you go along,
My heart waits for yours, watching
The clouds clear,
Just to open that star specked path
In the clear night,
Storms delay their light, what you have to do,
Is simple,
Uncover the beauty of your eyes, tilt
Your head up,
Let your eyes bring out, the brightest
Stars,
For when need be, I shall do,
Just the same.

Read Poetry More, Never Less

What would happen, if no one would read poetry?
If all, lost interest in her floetry,
Would poets loose their passion to write,
To stay within the dying of the light,
Or, would we rage,
Giving our poems another page
Never giving into death
Always around, to take another breath,
To disappear, or not to disappear
Only to reappear,
In a stronger way
We would write the day,
Give back passion to the night
We will continue to write,
In a time of emotional need
Poetry, we shall feed
To the mouths, of starving readers of life,
Ones, who want to run away from strife,
Loose yourself in rhyme
Forget about time,
Crack the spine, of a story in verse
When things get progressively worse
And all under a downpour of stress,
Read poetry more, never less,
Give poets inspiration to express
Read poetry more, never less,
Even if the world is in a mess
Read poetry more, never less,
Give us reason to write the moon
Don't wait, for poetry to be in ruin,
Give us reason to write the flower's bloom
Poetry shall not, meet its doom,

That light shall not go dim,
Nor will it die grim,
We shall stay above water so dark,
Express poetry in an open park
We the poets will stand,
Take young minds, by the hand
And lead them into a world of more,
Poetry book, sold out in every store
A dream we poets wish for,
But there stands a locked door
Denying the poets access
To poetic success,
They will feel the craving, for word in poetic flow,
The demand for poetry will grow,
To the world we must confess
For us, the poets, want you to read poetry more, never less.

To Silence

I wake in the busy streets of Manhattan
To silence,
Not a single rushing step is heard,
Only a rare, sound of a chirping bird,
Where are the honking cars
The millions of footsteps, moving at a speedy pace
Thinking life, is a rat race
To get high, in the ranks f their office,
But some are forever doomed
To work in a cubical,
Where they pound on their computer
Cursing life
Cursing bills
Cursing the world,
To silence
I wonder, where they are
Where's the two a.m. alarm of a car,
Where are the beggars and choosers
The bums and losers,
Begging for the "hard" earned money
Of passing executives,
Where are the street salesmen
Yelling out, five dolla five dolla
For a bootleg copy of a new theatre release,
And a fake nautical fleece,
Where are the people, that scream on the phone
While crossing the busy street,
Silence from the obnoxious sounds
Of the busy city life,
Where are all of those honks
And shrieks,
Heard, from the city's once highest peaks,

Now a burial ground of tears and sweat,
That we, can't ever forget,
To the silence
Of the aftershock,
That put Manhattan in a state of shock,
I live, in that block.

Two Way On A One Way Road

I feel my heart pounding,
Getting, faster and faster
With every passing second
It pounds, at a faster rate
Hard to swallow
Harder to breath,
I try to calm myself down,
But, there is no point in that,
I'm a disaster
Stuck inside a disaster site,
Can't breath right
Can't distinguish, between day and night,
How much time has passed
How much, of my life is gone,
Is that the sun or the moon
For my eyesight, is blurry,
Help!! Someone hurry
Get me out of this disaster,
That I myself did to my own heart,
I shook the tree that holds the winter's passing
And clouded my already cold mind,
I could not see, the figure, speeding toward me
Who is went the wrong way
Who picked the opposite route,
The burning flames creep closer to my dark attire,
My eyesight is clearing, for I can see
The opposite figure,
The tree shook, over him
Forgetting my need for aid,
I crashed into the sun drenched figure
For I went the wrong way
And bled, out the pain that resided,
I wear the proper attire, as the snow covered figure
Lives on to tell the story.

Gullible

Wait, I've heard this before,
Really can't take it anymore,
You'll say, that I will never happen again
I'll say, well then...
I'd think and come to the conclusion, its all right,
End to the argument, we'd go on with our casual night
There's a broken record here,
Don't know about you, but that what I hear
The hackneyed, excuse of it means nothing to him,
He sits in the lonely light, so dim
Only a fool would accept
His apology, why his mind, is only used to deceit
Those, who care about his heart,
While he tears others apart,
Pay close attention to this
He comes home, late, and gives a kiss
Her heart, is foolish and weak,
Something red on his cheek,
He had a late meeting at the office,
The early bus, he happened to miss,
Open your eyes
Stop believing those obvious lies,
One day, you will find out
But you'll just give it doubt,
Say he loves you too much
To give you, the coldest touch,
Don't trust his words of deceit,
And still you take your seat
Get up, and walk out that unlocked door
If you can't take it anymore,
For he'll be ready, with a lie
So that this relationship, shall not die,

There are better out there
For this guy is a glare
Distracting, you from something better,
Just leave, no need for a letter
He knows of his wrong
And knows he plays the same old song,
Walk out without him knowing
And your life, will keep flowing.

Originality

Have you ever heard, the words
Of one, with an original mind,
The depth, power, and imagery
Of what he speaks of, be blind
From the mind, of a madman,
Open, to the mind of inspiration
Speaking, to a small group
Or to an entire nation,
Through a powerful voice
Heard from, a song on a radio,
Now all you hear, is cursing
And shooting people up, at a studio,
Talking about the bling bling
And how their neck, needs to glisten,
It's to their corrupting words
That our kids listen,
Why should we kill,
For it happens, too many times,
Let's hear some originality
For I already heard, those rhymes.

The Mirror's Eyes

Its eyes can't see mine
For I am, invisible to the mirror's eyes,
Believe me when I say, I have no reflection,
I am noticed by living eyes
Also the eyes of the undead,
The mirror too scared to see me
To scared, to see my dark eyes,
The mirror's eyes won't even imagine
My eyes, for they are full of flames of hell,
Why would the mirror, be afraid of me,
The same reason why everyone else is,
My red blazing eyes, mirror hell
For I am the son of the Devil
And the kind, of the Un-dead,
Count Dracula, I do exist,
To the mirrors eyes, I don't
For the whole world, is a living mirror,
That is why no one can see me,
Invisible to the eyes of a mirror.

The Tall Glass

I know of an apartment,
A simplistic kind, in Manhattan,
Half the dresser, is empty
And the same stands the closet,
Two people, have been residing there,
For about two years
Always kept, clean,
Very nice tenants,
Last night, the building echoed with anger
As the two voices, were thrown around,
Shivered action of the halls and locks,
It all ended, with an unordinary door slam,
Traveled through the empty brown halls
Finding nothing, but the emptiness that surrounded,
There's a body o the floor
He's still alive, but sick,
An empty bottle next to him
And that bottle was his tall glass,
Where he buried his tears
Along with, the pain that suffocated him,
On the table lays two wine glasses
Empty of all that makes him smile,
He tried to drink, his problems away
But he wakes, to the repetitive song,
His tears overpowering his heart
He escapes, through the tall glass,
By himself, the apartment is dissimilar,
It sits grim on the island,
To get away
He finds, that tall glass,
Where he can run away
To face it, the next day,

Then to find, another tall glass
To run to,
A floating snowflake finds its way
Down, and begins to rest.

In The Depths Of Mid-Night

A breathless heart stares at the Dark Figure in disguise,
Its spidery legs approach the heart
That sits in a puddle, shaking in the winter warmth,
Two clouds shower blood as the heart kicks its covers.

Darkness will soon depart to Hell
But not before, a thunder strike upon the heart,
Not before a still, dark blue Ice,
A trembling leaf, in the Winter's Fall.

No where to turn
But into Darkness, truth,
The irritating chime, of a church bell
In the Morning sun, an open casket, a Wake.

History

What are the three wise men?
Will it also make me drunk? Shot number four,
What's my limit, before I'm too drunk and then
A total lapse in memory? Can I get a shot of Blackhouse?
I have fallen further into my drunken state,
But have not had, my face meet the floor
So, what is my limit? Should I even contemplate?
For I know now that the three wise men, are not wise at all,
And the real question is, is it my fault she's dead?

The Night After October 18th

There, I stand in the doorway with fear
By my side is the black cat,
With sympathy, blazing yellow, I hear
It speaks, a sudden outburst
To gain my attention, as I continue to stare
At a flickering candle, surrounded
In the vast bare
Darkness fills the emptiness of his room.

I can still see him
In the candlelight,
But its fading, for the fire has grown dim,
The cat walks into the room
And disappears, into the night sky,
I'm left alone standing in the doorway
With thoughts that will never die.

There Was Radio

Stories told,
Pictures, left to the imagination,
A box with a million voices
As all listened, to the breaking news,
Entertainment was heard at home,
Before the television
There was radio,
Giving people use of their brains
To imagine, how everything looked,
How a plump rose would be straining
Peaking its head, from the fire below,
Books were read at the RKO studio
People were scared, sitting in front of the radio
War of the Worlds was read,
Aliens had landed,
Funny to think, people though it news,
Now everything is right th4ree
The pictures are show,
Radio now only used for music.
But that to is fading into the shadows,
Why turn on the radio
When the TV, can show it all,
Leaving nothing, up to the imagination,
Imagine Sesame Street, on the radio
Your imagination would create Big Bird,
Theatres were starting to peak
Radio was diminishing,
People would go to the theatre, to see
See pictures of Hollywood
Radio was knocked out,
A strait jab, KO
Before television

There was radio,
Giving people an exercise,
There imagination was used
Don't sit so close, to the radio
It'll rot your ears?
Around the radio people gathered
Listening to soap operas, cartoons,
And movies
Adaptations, creating interest
Minds working to the max,
Images on a screen,
Versus creating them in the mind
Why think,
When you don't have to,
Why read the book,
When it is shown to you
Off-course, with some difference,
Radio was the source of entertainment,
To sit, and relax in front of the radio
To have your ears open to it
Open to the world,
How would it be
If there was not TV,
Pictures only thought of, in the mind,
Giving minds some exercise,
Before TV
There was radio,
Bringing the public stories,
Letting their imagination have fun.

Hidden Wings

Leaky drops echo through the
Closed off halls of a hospital,
Ten years of dust crowds
The darkened hall, of the hidden wing,
Those years, hide the truth
Of the same covered walls,
Stormy nights, bring light
Upon the darkened halls, within the
Strike of lightning, again, and again,
The shot of light breaks through
Its thick lies of dust,
One day, a gang of teenagers
Broke the lock, that kept the hidden wing
Closed and kept a secret for so many years,
They reach the door,
That sits chained with a lock at the heart,
With a fierce strike of steel,
Against steel, the lock breaks open,
As the door opens, a loud howl of wind
Rushes pass their ears,
Seven pairs of eyes stare out, into the black
Afraid to take, another step in,
Howling slaps of shots echo
In the throat, of the wing's rooms,
Two of the friends step
Shaking and scared,
Not even that far into the hall,
Claps of thunder and lightning
Distractions in the light
As the five struggle
In their continuous stairs,
Those two are gone from sight,

Blending in with the mystery of the night,
Six minutes later another pair of eyes walk in,
As the remaining four pairs watch,
Explosions, of thunder and simultaneous lightning
Strike over and over,
At first those eyes were not going to go,
But it was as if he was
Being called out into the dark,
Into the mystery of the night, the eyes disappear
Fourth pair of eyes takes a step,
Scared to be there,
Yet, he went thinking he'll be safer with the night,
A minute later, he decided to turn back,
Then a clap of thunder takes him,
The fifth pair of eyes runs in,
As if he was being chased,
Viscous red glowing eyes, behind his,
Over and over and over again, do those claps
Of thunderous strikes and blinding lightning
Takes him in further out,
The sixth and seventh pair,
As the seventh pair begs the sixth to leave
To go, something did not seem right,
The sixth pair, refused and went in
Looking for an escape in the thunder,
Then claps four times, gone,
A minute later, a silent thunder
Brings forward the devil,
The beast that took his six friends
And threw them into the night,
Never to return,
The seventh pair stood frozen,
As if his legs were broken,
Like a bullet,

The last pair of yes ran out,
And closed the doors
To the hidden wing, and the darkness
That lies endlessly behind them.

In Memory

I sit in a strange world, where space seems vast
Or so it seems through glass,
Some moments I live over again
Missing every peaceful moment,
Been through the same pain
Yet still, I don't remember my umbrella, I contain
Jumbles of thoughts and moments, a world twisted,
I sit tight fisted
Not understanding my life, and seconds that go by
Without me every fully going through a cry,
Never saw a movie at full length, I live moments,
Little sporadic dents
In a life I don't actually live, in memory
How can it be,
That the twisted world is slowly backing in
With a slight grin
Across its bank, it falls deep,
Around a pair of closed eyes it comes to creep,
Its words used to haunt
With words pressuring the heart, also to taunt,
A heart into a more twisted place of chaos,
In memory I sometimes cross
The depth of the dark blue ocean, staring eyes
Staring right at mine, picking, exposing, dies,
In memory I only see the blast,
I see the last
Of a life's seconds tick tocking away
Into no more night, no more day,
Darkness surrounds one second's tick of time,
In memory I live victim to a crime
Where thunderous sound echoes silent,
I live in a sleeping memory, living in a single dent.

Teacher

Six a.m. alarm clocks playing a waking tune,
Roads will be full of cars soon,
Dropping kids off, at school
And adults off to work, in their packed car pool,
One clock, sits with 6:01 glowing red,
Hurting eyes barley opens from its bed,
Bouncing eyes, going up and down the room,
Then, BOOM!
His alarm plays wake,
He gets up and squints at the sight of daybreak,
Begging for a few more hours of night,
Begging for darkness, to keep the sun out of sight,
He drags himself into the shower, to refresh his drowsy eyes
But, in a sense, he still lies
Sleeping comfortably in his pillow and cover,
He sluggishly walks out the door, leaving his lover,
His bed, alone it sits,
Its like the bed, can't live without him, it admits,
He starts his car and goes
For a feeling grows,
He shouldn't have left, never set foot,
Outside the door, outside he put,
His eyes at risk,
Almost forgot his saved essay, on computer disk,
Tinted covers to hide his hell raised eyes from being seen,
His fire sits around the centered green,
He enters the building, sensing all eyes on him
Shades show the building lights dim,
Shades of his eyes, never leave
For his right arm, also covered by his long sleeve,
Disguising his troubles, addiction, and illegalities,
His ears, hear the jingles of keys,

"Tommy, didn't expect you here, what's with the glasses."
No answer, every teacher in all his classes
He gets the same question and gives, the same response,
A small dance
Around the truth of his self caged eyes and arm,
That he cause's harm
To his own heart,
Stabbed with a needled dart,
Silence became his voice
As an addiction, was his only choice,
"Tommy, are you all right,
It's not that light
Please, take off the shades."
He pulls out the ace of spades
Painted, in the deviled red,
The teacher asked about his eyes, nothing, Tommy said,
He told his teacher nothing was wrong,
Asked to go to the bathroom, teacher said don't be long,
Tommy stared at the reflection,
Studied his pale complexion
And off color eyes,
Around his arm he ties
A rubber band,
The needled dart, held in his hand,
Squirt, push in the addiction,
He sits with his conviction
Floating round his head
And his eyes, lose the color red,
They turn pale green
Never, his true color to be seen,
Teacher knew, said, did
Nothing, his concern and worry hid.

Test Of Talent

Tapping foot on the cement
For the mind of a heart, has been bent,
Words echo in the night,
Test of talent, the mind will fight
The two hearts of the talented one
Till his crave for his creation is done,
Heart sits, starring at the flowing ink
Frozen eyes, scared to blink
Continuous to stare, at the soaked paper
As his mind, only pictures how evil raped her
And killed her beautiful blinking eyes,
He doesn't know, how to express his cries
His depression that has taken control,
Can't climb up the unfathomable hole
To where, he can write
And bring his mind out, from the dying of the light
He has sunk down too low
For words, to come into his usual flow,
His mind has been blocked
And in the center, lies a heart locked,
Talent tries to squeeze in
As Evil comes by with a grin,
Their eyes meet under the dark cloud
Test of talent is shouted out loud,
Leave my mind
Don't put my heart at blind
Sense the knowledge of rape and murder, the one without flaw
For I saw
Evil destroy her, Creativity,
Now no longer is she with me,
He screams out test of talent as Evil replies, his statement
As the tapping foot stops, on the cement,

"Swim deeper in your mind,
See what you can find
That will break the lock
That sits round your heart, ignore the tick tock
And listen to your heart beat,
Evil will be everything but, discrete."
Those words knocked hard, on the locked door,
Talent searched his core
Searching the deepest darkest depth
That leaves eyes without breath,
Talent found the key
In a thrown away memory.

Assassination of Royalty

The morning sun stretches its colors
Across the gray sky
Breaking through the dark covers
Of the fluttering eyes, sensitive to light,
He gets up as his eyes slowly adjust,
Walks to the balcony and stretches
His hands toward the sun rising colors,
Streaks of white clouds run
From one side of the earth to the other,
Os so it seems, by his Blue Eyes,
A loud thunderous clap
Echoes from ear to ear to ear
To the sun to the moon,
A man flows to the sunrise,
Successful assassination of Blue Eyes.
Listen, a story has to be told, has to be given
To the ravenous hearts and minds,
A fallen hero to the lifeless ordinary,
Where a schedule is followed religiously,
Every heart dormant,
Every pair of eyes, closed
And hidden from the wintered rose,
Blue Eyes was pushed into a life, confined,
Trapped in a schedule, hackneyed
In his own eyes, he knew
He was not living and was missing out,
Blue was taught the laws, rules, and ways
Of the ordinary hearts and minds,
Trapped in the religiously followed schedule,
He escaped into a schedule
With the freedom to choose,
His heart was trapped

In the way the moon is caged
In the gray rumbling clouds,
Blue saw how it was outside
The religiously followed schedule,
He was able to go beyond
The tortures confines of the Ordinary,
His eyes saw the sun fall and rise,
He saw the moon disappear and reappear,
Blue's heart lived to the emotion beat of the rain
And saw life, in a different mirror,
The Ordinary was a shattered piece
Of a hand made fake,
He knew others were blind
Behind the distorted colors of a simulated sunrise,
Blue Eyes spread his findings through
His testament,
The Ordinary tried to shut his eyes
Silence his truth,
And bring forth the religiously followed schedule,
Blue ignored them,
Revised his old testaments
That has been around for so long,
Blue went from gray cloud to gray cloud
Taking out the sun from its covers
And bringing forth its true sunrise,
After a year he invited
All who believed in life to a special meeting,
So many gathered in Venice, Italy
To see the most stunning sunrise,
With one thunderous clap
Blue Eyes was blinded yet again,
From sun to moon
All those hearts mourned
The savior of the lifeless ordinary.

Tear Shed

Onto the snow, tears bled
Out from the pounding shed,
Filled with false promises
The pair of eyes ran back with forehead and chest kisses,
She kept coming back for safety
Of a haunting memory,
She thought she'd find it behind the shed door,
After devoting so many years, tears still pour
Onto her own self, dirty, tired, and crying,
Her once vibrant eyes, were now dying,
Running still to her tear shed
Praying for forgiveness haunted memory floating in her hand
Her safe place rejected her,
She became the lost blur
For her prayers were stranded in her eyes and fears,
She lost her ears
By the sharp words from the home
She thought would always welcome with
Open arms, never to be a myth,
Always there,
Stare,
At the shed doors, locked to her heart
Right from the start
The shed was who she'd run to,
She grew
Up knowing that when problems arose,
Never would they look upon the dirt on her lying nose,
Whatever was done, can't be taken away
Till the chaotic, distraught, and wide open day,
Her tears were shed and taken, never to return
In favor, her urn
Was never spilled, brushed into a pale,

Never to set sail,
To splendor of an open peace,
The shed stole every piece
Of her devoted life, only to the shed,
Where millions of hers and trillions of other tears bled,
Ringing bell heard by her eyes
In the blue sky and sun rising colors, she dies,
Finally an end to her struggle,
The sharp words poked at her life's protective bubble
And opened her to the end,
The shed and other sheds were certainly not a godsend
But a destruction of nature and smile,
She walks a different mile,
Collecting back her tears
And loosing her haunting fears.

The Roof

Why do I sit here looking at
Stars and a moon that never shined bright for me,
I sit here on the high top
Living, in what seems to be,
An endless non-living night
That gives no shadowed moon,
To my ears and nose
I can feel sunrise comes soon,
Never to show its vibrant colors
Streaking across itself,
I beg for my eyes to open
And release the dust from their resting shelf,
My world is a pitch black,
Never ending night
That has no moon nested
In a bed of trillions upon trillions of stars, blind sight
Constant and grueling
Are those battles within my own dying heart
As I stretch my hands up
Hoping to touch the midnight part,
I am the howling wolf
Crying for the moonlit sight
Crying from vision
Of the pitch black midnight,
I'm cursed in darkness
For committing sin,
Cursed for committing
Something I don't feel within,
It pokes around my heart,
Like the prickling thorns of a rose,
I try to escape my curse
But the so-called heavenly doors stay in its pose

No where to run
As I plant myself on the roof,
The sin I am cursed for
Is the shadowed spoof,
But here I sit
Crying for the vision,
I wait till I awake,
Just in time, to see day and night, in collision.

The Second's Kiss

What do my eyes see in the far distance,
A vision blurred, by the falling snow
I'm trapped in place, for what feels like an instance,
Trapped in the heavy white flow,
I see an angel, behind the white mist
Of winter's waterfall, a snowy image
Frozen in sight as the second kissed,
Time is sending love, a valued message,
Do my eyes lead me into her
Heart that is still in place,
I fall out of the kiss, no more does my sight blur,
I escape my frozen keep, and see her angelic face,
I enter the mist and feel the second,
For the brief measure of time's kiss, is destined.

Tortured Through Windows

I point my tortured heart up at the sky
Not expecting the clouds to cry,
I look through my blue windows
Watching for when the storm wind blows
Of the devil's ferocity,
It hurts when it touches, I'm curious,
Why do I feel tortured pain
Every time storm clouds bring wind, not rain.

A little boy sits, face stuck to the rain soaked
Window, pouring streaks from the storm, day has choked
Of grey clouds, they hover
Around the house of gloomy eyes,
You could see sadness in disguise,
A mask to cover a conspiring grin,
Through blue windows bodies walk, in sin
Hanging over their hearts,
Tortured are they and their counter parts,
The little boy wants to go outside,
On a clear day, where he doesn't have to hide,
Shades drawn like the slim moon in the clear night sky,
Look from out to in, little boy holds his cry,
The Little Boy is tortured behind
The drawn shades, are to cover the mind,
Tortured through windows of blue,
I wear it on my bare arm, as pain grew
Only to find another pair of windows
Who protects when a cloud grows,
Ease to my torture, behind drawn shades,
My hearts permanent aid.

The Distant Hearted

Un-restful in her distracted fears,
Through her shut lids, come seeping out, her tears,
A heart lies in bed, under attack,
Tears fall from the sky dressed in black,
Two hearts fear the fall season
For the distancing reason.

A bed centered in a room
In a house, a heart in un-rested ease,
"I love her to the depth of my heart
Why do I fear I'll lose her love
In the fall, when her bags, packed
And ready for higher learning,
She loves me, her fallen tears prove her worry
That she might lose my heart,
She'll be gone and I'll be here
Sitting, in the tear
That drops to blue waters,
I don't want to lose her,
My sweet Night Shade, to the distance,
I can't lose her to what lies
In between my heart and hers."

Phone rings in the low light
Of the vacant room, with only
Poetic Heart, on the bed,
He jumps to answer thinking
It might, just might be her.

"Sorry, wrong number."
Poetic lays back down
With the same thoughts, running by his side,

Resting his head on the pillow,
In through the window
Comes the moons full glow,
Tomorrow she leaves
Told by the falling leaves,
Next morning Poetic makes his way
Over to her heart, and there she is
On her bed, off to the right, in a room, un-rested,
In a house, un-rested.
"It can't be today, too fast
It comes, too fast are the summer months,
I don't want my eyes to flutter open,
Rather they stay shut, that way
No acknowledgement of a dreaded day,
Alarm clock rings, time to depart,
But how do I tell my heart
That we have to have love in distance,
I can't be the distant hearted,
Why does it beat so fast,
It's like it knows, already aware,
That the fallen leaf, has touched down
And turned, to the fallen color, my frown
Used to be different, full and green,
Far reaching roads, in between
Love, comfort, and ease on me."

Poetic walked up to Night's front door
With his heart beating fast
And so hard, ready to burst out of his chest,
She opened, and both their hearts
Chilled in the cool breeze
Of their blue windows,
Their arms wrapped around each other tightly
Never wanting to let go,

Night' eyes started to lose control
As well as her heart and mind,
She started to cry, slowly
Since she tried so hard to hold back.

"I'm scared, I didn't want to wake up,
I…I don't know what else to say,
I've grown speechless."

While looking into Night Shade's eyes
Poetic told her, in a gentle voice,
"You don't have to say anymore,
There is nothing to fear, I won't lose you
To the distance between our hearts,
I love you too much to let space
Separate us, take us apart,
It can't, it won't destroy our love
For this I have never been so sure,
Believe my words are truths
I give you, my Poet's honor
That I won't, lose you
And you won't lose me in the far
Distance, for our eyes will see the same night
And our hearts will beat at the highest bright,
Believe me, my heart, mind, body
For your love, is my poetry,
The brightest verse in the darkest poem,
I will always, always love you."
They hugged tightly, staying in each others arms,
Hours passed, and Night had to go,
A ride along the river's flow
And Poetic, back to his bed,
There he lays in a bed, in a room, in a
Distracting house, in a chaotic world

Thinking about Night Shade,
How much he loves her, and how much
He wants her in his life,
She's too young to know if she wants him
For the rest of her life,
He needs distraction, from distance
From his love, the distant hearted,
But nothing could throw her
From his mind filled with her,
Days to weeks to months,
End of the fall semester,
There she sits an anxious heart, watching
As she gets closer to her love back home,
They see each other, and it is the same
Love, if not stronger.

"I missed you so much, I thought
The semester would never end."
"I did as well Poetic."
"I have a question, how long do you
Want my heart, my love, me for?"
For as long, as I could have you."
For a long time, my love will always, always
Be in yours, in your loving arms,
I want you in my life."

The Picture of Sanity and Insanity

I sit there, straining to concentrate
Upon the lecture, that has my hour,
But this picture, has taken my focus,
A sky packed clouds, could be night
Or it could be a gray
Day in the life of sanity, and insanity,
Clouds painted in passionate burgundy, with shades
Of Darkness, and then the storm clouds,
Overtaken by insanity puffs,
Insanity comes from the heart,
Not the mind, it just recites emotion,
Insanity is a woman, in my case,
Sunlight of the broken sky, she surrounds
My thoughts of pain, diminished
Once light of her smile, word, touch
Graces my circle, she is my insanity,
And I want to commit,
A knock upon my heart, I've let insanity in.

Haunted Heart

A dim apartment all day and night
A heart lays in the corner, balled in fright,
For the shades are drawn blocking out the day
And the moon, that out to play,
The heart lays haunted of the repetitive past,
Of a love, that did not, could not flow, too fast
The love came and went, love still felt
In the hearts, a feeling that would instantly melt
The life off of him,
Love haunts his heart, tearing the high light, to dim
Low in the lively day, even lower in the moon,
Invisible love sits beside, leaving soon
To only reappear over and over again, to haunt, to interrupt
His life, and to erupt
His passionate moon imbedded in the starry sky,
A feeling he can't realize, needs to die,
Three knocks on the door,
He can't get up off the mattress off the floor
Screaming go, not to bother his thought,
He was caught,
His friends knew what conquered his mind, and lingered bout,
The lost love that should have never been, a shout,
Leave, leave me within my love, which sat in his mind,
One he always tired to find,
Concerned are they, never do they see his heart
For in the drawn night, it is being torn apart,
By the, haunted love that lives in the night.
His love comes to him in dark light
For it is attracted to the dark reflection,
In his mind, sits a collection
Of images, picturing him and her
That can lure

His heart into a deeper hurt,
Which he sees as comfort,
Reality blinded in the cracks of a shadow
The moon, blocked out, shades blind the vibrant glow
That used tom hit his heart
And soothes his body part,
That beats for her touch,
The image of his mind has a tight clutch
In his weak heart, breaking him down,
The image always appears in her long white nightgown
To show, it is always night, always dark
In his apartment, a wide open park
Now limited by her,
Half his head is a complete blur
Which is happens to be reality,
Haunted by a love he used to see
At the end, of a long day, he saw her at night
With absolutely no light
Coming in, to his now closed eyes,
Care and concern, the sun tries
To bring him back
And take him away, from a pitch black
World, bring him into the moonlit
Sky and passionate
Life, he once had, without his love image,
His friends all climbed onto the ledge
And brought the haunted heart, down slowly
Setting, the moon to run free.

Young Eyes

Sweet dreams baby boy,
Lights off, except for the night light
Tucked in the far corner of the room,
Slowly the boy slips into a deep
But not so, relaxing sleep,
His young eyes close and fall
Into his nights rest,
Not too long before dreams
Come to life, one filled with screams
Of fear and pain,
In the dream he stands in a far corner
Watching his mom, laying on the floor,
Bottles crashing, splattering alcohol
As his eyes turn to the noise,
His father in another drunken state,
All of a sudden, the father stops
And meets eyes with the boy,
The father starts a charge toward the corner
Of shining light, pulls back his hand
Ad lets go, full swing ahead
Dream stops, out from his head,
Young eyes, stay open for the rest of the night.

Next night, sweet dreams baby boy,
Lights off, except for the night light
Tucked in the far corner of the room,
A dream, comes up again
The same with a little variation,
The father is of a clear mind
Hitting the mother repeatedly
As she lays, motionless on a cold floor,
Baby boy, now with some bruises

Under his right eye and the left side
Of his lower lip,
Blood from both goes, drip, drip
As his father, uses his hand to smack,
Uses it to crack
The gentle silence of the house
And of baby boy's dreamland,
Once again baby boy, wakes from dream
This time, from his own scream,
Next night, sweet dreams baby boy,
Lights off except for the night light
Tucked in, the far corner of the room,
Young eyes stayed open
To think about, when he dreamt sweet,
When his father was gone,
Before he came home,
His mother said, he left ten years ago
When those young eyes
Peered out, into the world,
Dreams are chaotic and violent
Too much, for young eyes,
Before those eyes closed to sleep
His mother came in, packing quickly, silently,
Baby boy, and ran,
Now young eyes close, to his
Sweet dreamland.

The Never Loving Family

In a heart sits an ocean
Filled, to the deep end of an emotion,
That was never fished out, never expressed,
After forty years, I am dressed
In the nightly color, to say farewell
For without love, my family shall dwell,
I remember sporadic moments of my childhood,
I wish I could
Never remember anymore,
A fistful hit knocks me out, on the cold never loving floor,
Those are the kinds of memories, which stick around
Me lying hurt on the ground,
Everyday, I see tons of families
Living with love, storing good memories,
I lived in a house I wanted to run away from
Wanted more, than just a crumb
To feed, my heart every night
In the covered moonlight,
If pain was their love, they loved me too much
For I feared, their loving touch,
Whenever they were near,
I flinched in fear
Hoping I could run away, from it all
But I would suffer, my whole self would fall
Until they would find me, and take me back,
A repeating crack
Of the genuine leather belt,
Whipping my skin, was what I felt,
At age ten, I run toward the moon
Knowing, soon
I'll smile for the first time
No longer sublime
But real, in my heart,
I found love, in love with poetry's art.

Dead Tree, Broken Sidewalk

Every kid fears, that poky looking house
At the end, of their peaceful block,
That haunted mansion that they dare
Their,
Friends to go in, and check it out,
On a different end of a different block
Is a tree, and its sidewalk,
Not only kids, but teens, adults, and elders
Fear its grim sight,
S dead tree and a broken sidewalk
With roots poking out,
From under it,
The elders say, a boy was lost
To that tree, taken by the sidewalk
And fed to the dead tree
At first, no one believed the elders
Thought they were fabricating
Just to scare, the little block,
Wasn't funny, when a non-believer
Disappeared, lost to the dead tree,
His camera found, near it,
A picture was taken, of the boy
Getting sucked in,
So in those haunted houses
No evidence, no truth
Can be presented,
A path of tress leading, up to
A specific one, a grim one,
No leaves to cover its branches,
It stands high only,
To point back down.

"I don't believe it, no such thing
Can happen, a tree eating people."

"Its true, I was the one who took the picture,
I saw it happen,
He stepped on the sidewalk, and sunk in,
I got so scared, that I dropped the camera
And ran home, I'm serious,
Never have I seen something so frightening,
The tree is the entrance to hell,
That is why it points down."

"Kill the tree, break it from where it stands,
Then no more, will people be eaten."

"You can't, for you'll let in, something,
Someone,
That should be, left out."

The Broken Quill

Frantic, he runs through the town
Looking for help, someone to help,
"Please help me!"
No one turns a single eye, in his direction
No one stops him, says calm down, no one,
His quill is broken, he can't write,
Continues to run with his quill
In his right hand, close to begging,
Down, on hands and knees,
Without his quill, he can't write.
He can't express, his mind,
Without it, he's a poor blind,
Frantic man, looking for an answer in candlelight,
Someone has blown it out,
Torture, to words,
He returns to his empty flat,
A desk pushed all the way, to the back wall
Of a narrow room, his writing hall,
It faces his only window
Where he can see inspiration,
No more, for the paper lays empty
Missing, his words of light,
Words, sentences, whole books come into his head
But his hand, lies dead
On the floor, of the long narrow hall,
No life runs, through its fingers,
The broken quill, lies in two,
One, a few inches, away from his cold hand
And the other, on the window sill,
No more words in tears, from the quill
Unless, someone will turn his way,
He was writing, a story that

Might have been, his greatest,
Angelic words in their feathered flow
Onto the quill, this now lies broken,
He was writing nonstop
That even a thunderclap, couldn't bother,
Except the crack,
Now a mind under attack
With continuous words,
Nothing in his hand, he can't put words
Into love, passion, a crime,
His head holds his crimson, rhyme,
His eyes open and sees, the full moon,

"Take me, crush my hand
So I don't itch to write,
Explode my mind and set those
Words, sentences, books free
From me,
Please, take me away so I am no longer
In burden, of the missing words,
Let me feel the breeze
From the deep waters, of the ocean,
Take away my need, crave, emotion
To write, onto my empty pages,
Take me now, for I have no one,
That can help."
He stares down at the tip, of the quill,
Slit, slit, no more words, sentences,
Or even, books.

Framed Decisions

A dying man lies in bed, while his hand
Is held by his mind clouded granddaughter,
Heavy breaths disturb his sleep
For he could never fall too deep,
Tears soak, the bed
That come from, young green eyes,
The dying man whispers
Into the ear, of his loving granddaughter,
He asks her,
"Did I ever tell you, a story?"
The granddaughter shook her head no
While, wiping away tears,
"Well, let me tell you one,
There lived a woman, full of life
She was about to embark
On a journey, to better herself,
She was excited to go, but then she was saddened,
For she had to leave behind the people
She cared so much for,
Used to the way things were, how everyone
Was so close to each other,
Her heart began to ache, worried too much
She was having, a tiny feud with,
Her mother,
A woman who had already planned out
The rest of her daughter's life
That could mirror her own, the life
Of the mother, only with a tiny twist,
The daughter would achieve, what the mother couldn't,
The daughter was confused
For an unexpected love, came and eased
Her worried and aching heart,

She loved his so much
That she had, no reason to leave,
Too late, a decision was made, and she was leaving,
But love would last between the two,
Phone calls, love letters they wrote,
The daughter changed her mother's plans
And went, to a different profession,
The tiny feud, grew, rumbled in thunderous
Shadows, for it only struck when another reason
Arose in the stage light,
What the mother didn't expect, was all these
Bottled up words, and framed life decisions
Would drive her away,
But the man the daughter was in love with
Was the same mind,
He showed the mother, that her daughter
Needed to be her own person,
For her heart desired something
That the mother could not wait for,
Love, true love
That eased pain, worry, and heartache,
The frame was broken
Since the daughter's heart grew too big,
If a heart grows past an unexpected height,
You have to give it room."

The hand of the dying man started to weaken,
As tears grew in the eyes of the granddaughter,

"Your grandmother, was an extraordinary person
That gave my heart, an extra inch
After it stopped growing."
Flat line, the man passed with his granddaughter's
Eyes, open wide in his.

In the Shadow of the Gun

I can't look into the eyes
That lie in the shadow, of the gun,
He sees my eyes, full of fear
Never from the shadows, does he appear,
Hidden, he stays to conceal his identity,
Hidden, is the light that hides
The one, that pumps fear into my heart,
Every time, my eyes close,
The gun shows
Up to frighten me, and hark back,
In the shadow of the gun, I stare,
For the voice behind it
Shakes me, takes my heart
Under its power,
Whose eyes, voice, and hand that holds the gun
Lives in, that shadow
Hiding himself from the light
That shines his eyes free from night,
I have no face, to put with fear
Nothing but a gun, and darkness
As its controller, its handler,
Its that moment that won't leave
My mind, never without it
For it belongs to that tick in time
Where my heart, dropped to fear,
And where my eyes, dropped every single tear
Till no more, remained,
Till that gun, disappeared into its shadow,
When my eyes close
I live it I see it I feel it I hear it all,
All over again, to put fear back in,
Watching over my shoulder
Whenever I step,

Never feeling safe, not at home
And not in the comfort of my bed,
Shadows lie in the corners of my mind
Hiding till that moment
Where my eyes close, then to appear
Is that all too, familiar fear,
The shadow of the gun
And the trigger, that ends the dream.

The Yearning Paper

Picture a room, not a big one
No windows for the moon or sun
To enter at its peak, the color blue painted
On the walls, a desk constrained
To the room, with no air to breath, no world to see,
On a desk, a blank paper, for words are a distant memory
For the paper lives alone, on the at the far end,
Now lend
Your ears and listen, to what echoes off the walls
For there is no escape, into the moonlit halls,
No entrance, closed to every single heart
Unfortunately, the paper can't tear itself apart
Ending its misery, for without words of love or pain,
What else is there, yearning for a mind that might contain
Those words that might fill up the page,
No longer will it age
No longer will it yearn, in the darkness of the room,
Where not even the slightest thought, can bloom,
Now imagine fifty years
And no longer, can your ears
Hear, the yearning paper, the blue paint has chipped away
Disclosing its ugly color gray,
Darkness controls the room's, silent walls,
For darkness controls, the mind's silent halls.

Out of Reach Memory

I slowly wake, as my eyes push open
And take in the dim light, dulled by gray clouds,
I sit up, and rest my head against a picture frame,
The people in the snapshot, I can't recall their names
Or who they are to me, they've become lucid faces
And hazy in the snowy distance, unable to reach
For that memory, as it slips away, second by day,
Used to be able to remember easier, no hesitation
And would not blank on a name or place,
My memories have begun to be out of reach,
Soon, I'll forget my own name, my own face,
Wake up one day, look in the mirror and say,
Who are you? I'll try to have a conversation
With my own reflection, only, I won't know its me,
For my own image, will be a lost memory,
And I'll go mumbling on, asking over and over,
Who am I? I remember hearing once,
That nascence, in the mind, bliss, would you agree?
I don't, absence is fright, waking up every morning
Not knowing, who you are, where or what,
My wife died three years ago, my favorite memory of her,
Is slowly fading away, soon it'll be a blur,
Trying so hard to recall, what was I saying?
Oh yea, its that easy to forget, now that
My mind has slipped, into the dusty sheds
Of memory's lot, which I visit frequently
As I lay emptied, mumbling over and over,
That one question, I can't answer anymore,
For I have become, that out of reach memory,
Who am I?

A Nameless Street

I know where I am, but then again, I don't,
Can't make out the buildings
Can't read the blank green street signs,
The sidewalks are cracked and has no life to it,
No trees, but a chalked outline,
A black rose on the corner of the sidewalk
With nothing, written on the street sign,
Its early in the morning, the sun will soon rise
And perhaps bring light upon where I am,
All that surrounds me is blurred, has my vision gone,
I don't know where to go
What I'm even doing here,
It all seems so unreal but at the same time,
It feels too real, familiar feelings
Vague buildings and landmarks
A nameless street, has me lost,
In the darkness that surrounds this one street,
Among the few people that walk the street
Faces blurred, off course, there is one
Straining to make out the face,
As I get closer, the picture gets clearer
My heart beats faster and faster,
This is a dream, it has to be a dream,
Non of this is real, I want to wake up,
I don't want to be here anymore
Let my alarm go off so that my eyes will open
And take in true reality, somebody wake me up,
This isn't real, you're dead.

Blind Steps

I've decided to stay back, not to go any further,
To let my steps to be blind,
You're probably wondering why, if there is a way
For my sight to return, why not take it,
I love the sight of the night sky
Where the moon is embedded in trillions of stars,
But I take bind steps,
The striking sight, of her smile
But I take, blind steps,
The snow covered palace, Central Park
But I take blind steps,
So I can't see murder and war,
"Seeing is believing", and I rather not,
I'll listen out for the howl of a wolf
And I'll know, the full moon is out,
I'll feel the weather bite, and cold wet feathers
Fall onto my face, as I face the heavens
And I'll hear her smile, for its that obvious,
But I do confess, I'll miss the sights,
While taking, those blind steps.

Lured In

She took him by the hand
With her big beautiful green eyes,
He had no idea where they were, he said I'll just stand
Still, she continued to lure him in as the light dies
From the room behind, only the light, from the room ahead
It the hall they were walking down,
A thought, kept circling, "What would happen, if I fled?"
Would she show tears along side, a deep frown
He tried so hard to pull away
But her grip was too strong to break,
She turned her eye to his, softly said, "stay"
With that, she lured him, into sleep, never to wake,
An odd smile, upon his face,
Was it too fast a pace?

A Bright Day After a Moonless Night

A startled heart, jumps from their dream world,
Only ten minutes of sleep,
A patient heart waiting for an angel
To come and sleep by its side,
A tear sneaks out, from the corner, of his eye
Heavy and rapid breaths, wide eyes
Looking from the left to right, pitch black night sky,
A flower without its bud, nothing for eyes to reflect,
Slower breaths, eyes straining to stay open,
Tossing and turning, kicking the cover
As if it's a rabid dog attacking, the heart
Jumps out from their dream world, with a startled word,
The ears of the walls shake, the heart trembles
Uncontrollable dreams and images hold
The heart in a tight cell, of nightmares,
It searches for the bright moon in complete darkness,
Only to find, nothing, unable to see without it
The heart falls, into that feared dream world,
Startled words, fly from the heart, still asleep
But this time, the heart can't escape
The grasp of this dream world,
A patient heart, no longer has to wait,
An angel takes it away from the haunted sleep,
An everlasting brightness, after a moonless life.

In the Atmosphere

What evil lurks about, in the after
Midnight hours, a pain present
A feeling Resigned, the Garden
Numbness comes over a Heart, swimming in shadow,
He stands in the middle of the Dearly Departed
Pouring out tears, onto those Good and Evil,
Deathly winds Bite at those already tortured
Still, that heart never moves, no shiver
From the Cold touch upon his shoulder
Darkness shows its Light, after the midnight hour
As Howling winds rush round the Atmosphere,
The heart's Permanent Visit to the Garden.

Insanity's Welcome

Do you know, what I did last night,
I drove home, then sat in the car,
I didn't go right inside, I opened up the moon roof
And starred outside, at the night sky
Starred at the stars, that starred right back down at me,
Open bare to my eye scattered all over,
Looking for its king, Moon,
Lost without him, dependant on its light
To show the way to the true heart,
Its sad to think that some, mistake the night, for fear,
Those are the sane ones, for insanity
Brings much more than fear,
The night is the domain, where insanity dwells,
What is sanity, and are we sane?
Insanity comes from the heart not the mind,
For it is the heart that gives you these crazy notions and feelings
You can't ignore,
. Sadness, depression, happiness, anger, love, passion
Are all part of insanity beats that you hear, if you listen to
your heart
That pounds heavy and as loud as it can,
Some listen, as some don't
Just like some stare at the stars,
And some just ignore it, or use
The absence of the moon, to hide in shadow,
Insanity is peace, creativity, wild imaginations, and sparks
In the soul of a person, who has entered the gates.
The moon is the gateway to it
For it is the other eye of a higher being,
It is sane to follow religion, schedule, and stupidity
For there are better ways, happier and life fulfilling,
Where can one go, if the clouds block our gates

From sight, where to run from sanity blades,
Take time, from your busy schedules of praying
An giving up, what you love
To point, your windows up
To let your heart breathe,
If not, it will suffocate and the mind
Will bring sanity, to your heart.

The small decisions in life are not concrete,
They are merely Jell-O, so break in.

Giant And A Mouse

Out my window
Smiles glow,
Life has a happy flow
For on my face, there is no
Smile to mirror my life.

I hear the lock turn
As I burn
My smile and hide
Under the shaking covers,
My room turns to darkness
As his footsteps near,
I am a mouse
And my father is a giant,
The belt buckle jingles
In the still silence
A hug from the whip, named violence
Violet colored skin,
Do I dare stay?

I hear the lock turning
For my first thought,
Is, where do I hide,
Under the bed
In the closet,
Just for one night
To escape pain,
But hiding my whiskers,
Won't help, he knows my places,
He loves to tease me
Pick me up by my tail
And hang me over a boiling pot,

Punishing me,
More like pushing me away,
As long as he doesn't hurt me
But, who am I kidding,
That bottle will not be sitting
As it holds his drug, full lot.

The lock turns
Then I freeze, freeze, freeze,
As he comes in,
A six year old mouse, a child
Scared to be wild,
His angry eyes see my
Eyes full of innocence,
All I want is a kiss on the forehead
Or a hug, from the heavy footed giant,
But all I feel
Are arms of his pure leather whip,
Wrapping round me
A defenseless little animal
Tortured by the giant,
Just because he can
He leaves bruises of love on me,
No, I don't feel it,
I feel the hurt,
All I want is a kiss on my forehead, or a hug,
For the giant to make friends
With the house mouse,
But the bottle is the only one
That gets love from the beastly giant,
The bottle is hugged
By his two lips
And held, tight in his hands
An inescapable grip,

And much more than just a sip,
For he hits his own,
I try to get away
Far from his hit.

I hear the lock, turning
As the bottle keeps spinning
In the tears of green,
Closer and closer do those footsteps
Come, his hand hangs off the couch
Waving at the floor
That only holds fallen tears,
Silently, the door unlocks,
With a thunderous slam,
A closed book, of a thousand pages,
For no more will the mouse sit
In another obvious hiding place.

I can't run from his harmful swing
Inside the door to my home,
Never can I feel safe,
For I feel safer, here on the streets
With the rest, of the mice.

Featured poet, Sadie Ryczek

Deceptions

Through broken shards and falling pieces
the reflection of a tattered face
through dark red eyes and falling tears
the feeling of relief
through broken promises and harsh cruel words
the loss of all feeling

the mind drifts to calm peace
while the body falls away
slowly down from the soul
all pain melts to nothing
throughout the flow

blot away the hurt with a tissue
wipe the tears with your sleeve
put on the smile and pretend it isn't there
all will be ok
if you just hide it all away

a loss of self

The snow falls gently
as the fireplace gleams
the space you once filled now empty
holding the blanket tight
hoping to feel the warmth we once shared
the pictures on the mantle are just as they were
not one smile out of place
and yet I wish it wasn't so
you've grown so distant
I barely know who you are now
The person you've become is not the person I once loved
but how can that be?
how can one person change so fast...

Miquela

Bright smiles and young blue eyes
the youthful glow we all once had
genuine joy at the smallest things
a little girl growing up so fast
the innocence in every smile
tears shed for the lost teddy bear
giggles at a butterfly
songs about sunshine and lollipops
screams about a closet monster
such youth and innocence
to be inevitably lost to time
watching her grow I worry for her future
I hope not all that innocence escapes her
the joy and hope I see in her
my beautiful baby niece

nightmares

familiar hands
a painful touch
hurtful words
hot breath
forceful arms
pressing down
pushing hard
on a small body
hard motion
racking tears
shaking the soul
rough hands
tearing flesh
violent movement
ripping apart youth
silent screams
choking words
falling hard
onto the floor
curling up
to try to hide
gripping tight
a soft quilt
forcing out
painful words
closed eyes
tightening with each memory
stay awake
push them out
terrifying nightmares
time and again

comfort

hide away
dry your eyes
don't let them see the hurt inside
no one knows
what's hidden there
even though they say they care
but just then
a glimpse of hope
when you feel you just can't cope
a gentle hug
a tiny kiss
everything you really miss
that smiling face
a hand to hold
makes you feel you're not alone
just the words
you need to hear
show then just a tiny tear
they make you laugh
let yourself smile
a quiet escape just for a while
those terrible thoughts
creeping in
the flood of tears starts again
lean your head
on a comforting shoulder
helps you feel a little stronger
you're not alone
you know it now
they're here to stay they truly vow
And though you're scared
and though you cry
they hold you tight, they're by your side.

Uncomfortably Numb

I fall to fast
I fall to hard
I let myself feel all too much
I block the tears
I hide the pain
but every day it gets harder
The tears push their way past
my eyelids shut oh so tight
Lost in the whirlwind of confusion
Not knowing where to turn anymore
the ground falls away from beneath my feet
I reach out for a helping hand
only to find that had slipped further away
I push too hard
I hide too much
but it's plain as the nose on my face
but you don't care
or so you say
yet you push so hard back at me
is it time
is it hate
is it love that drives us apart
do I even want to know the answer?
So much said and so much learned
yet what was it all for in the end?
for everything to come crashing down?
maybe I asked for it...

Breinigsville, PA USA
02 December 2009
228532BV00004BA/48/A